HATCH
MATCH
&
DISPATCH

HATCH
MATCH
&
DISPATCH

A CATHOLIC GUIDE TO
SACRAMENTS

RICHARD LEONARD, SJ

Paulist Press
New York / Mahwah, NJ

Jacket images from Bigstock.com, top to bottom: by VAKSMANVM, by maximkabb, by doigachov
Jacket design by Dawn Massa, Lightly Salted Graphics
Book design by Lynn Else

Library of Congress Cataloging-in-Publication Data:
Names: Leonard, Richard, 1963- author.
Title: Hatch, match, and dispatch : a Catholic guide to sacraments / Richard Leonard, SJ.
Description: New York, NY : Paulist Press, [2019] | Includes bibliographical references.
Identifiers: LCCN 2018026554 (print) | LCCN 2018045636 (ebook) | ISBN 9781587687686 (ebook) | ISBN 9780809106509 (hardcover : alk. paper)
Subjects: LCSH: Sacraments—Catholic Church.
Classification: LCC BX2200 (ebook) | LCC BX2200 .L465 2019 (print) | DDC 265—dc23
LC record available at https://lccn.loc.gov/2018026554

ISBN 978-0-8091-0650-9 (hardcover)
ISBN 978-1-58768-768-6 (e-book)

Published by Paulist Press
997 Macarthur Boulevard
Mahwah, New Jersey 07430

www.paulistpress.com

Printed and bound in the United States of America

To Frank & Ruth, Alice & Jack, Dympna & Tomas, Cliodhna, Pat, Roisin, Mary, Annie & Padraig, Craig & Julie, Marisa & Simon, Colleen & Mike, Tammy & John, Adam & Nicole, John, Chris & Stephen, Adele & Christian, Susan, Christine & John, the Hughes family, the Morahan family, the McGinness family, Cordelia, Sidonie & Sebastian, Helen & Mary, Cate, Samm & John with many thanks for all the grace-filled moments we have shared

Contents

Acknowledgments

Mark-David Janus, CSP, Paul McMahon, Bob Byrns, and the team at Paulist Press for their continuing belief in me and my work, and for enabling me to talk to a very wide audience about faith and culture;

Brian McCoy, SJ, and the Australian Province of the Society of Jesus for the education and formation I have received and their ongoing support to do the "greatest good for the greatest number";

Rev. Dr. Stephen Hackett, MSC, and the Australian Catholic Bishops Conference, who understand that the ministry of communication involves various forms of the presentation of the Word;

The forbearance of my Jesuit community at Lavender Bay, Sydney, whose support and care, at home and while away, provide a home base for a ministry often lived "with one foot in the air."

Introduction

BOOKS on the sacraments generally fall into three categories: catechetical material for children; material for adults often preparing for the sacraments of initiation; or scholarly theological volumes. I am hoping that *Hatch, Match, and Dispatch* bridges all three categories. While it reflects careful research and often summarizes very complex history and arguments, it is not written for the academy. I hope it will be a useful resource for teachers preparing children for the sacraments as well as adults on the journey of coming into the life of the church. Moreover, I hope it will be an engaging primer, or a refresher, for Catholics and other Christians who want to know why we have these seven moments of God's grace, how we came to have them in the form we presently celebrate them, and what they mean for us as they mark the visible signs of our invisible God.

My other intention in writing this book is that we recover the truth that our sacraments, when celebrated well, are among our preeminent tools for evangelization. As good as many evangelization programs are, it is true that the times when most people come to church on our terms is for a hatching, matching, or dispatching, and many are open to hearing a hopeful word that speaks to the joy or sadness they bring with them. Indeed, it would be wonderful if the warmth of the welcome they receive as well as the attention to the dignity, beauty, and flow of the sacrament might enable them to ask some of the deeper questions and seek the answers about life's meaning and the grounds for faith toward which the sacrament is already pointing and making real. If every parish thought of every baptism, wedding, and funeral, in fact, all the sacraments, as opportunities to witness to the faith, hope, and love they signify, it could have a dramatic impact on how we celebrate Christ's sacraments and the invitation to new life to which each of them invites us.

Additionally, given that we are celebrating these sacraments in Christ's name, whose real presence is accessible in and through them, we might recall where, how, and to whom Jesus especially went while on earth. His ministry was regularly with people who did not tick all the religious boxes of his day. He praised, gave as role models, or took words and actions of healing, welcome, and new life to non–temple-going shepherds, Jewish tax collectors, women with bad reputations, notorious sinners with whom he dined, lepers, and those whom were considered ritually unclean. If this were good enough for the Lord, why would his approach not be good enough for us?

Regarding the entire mission of the church, as well as our sacramental commission, Pope Francis states, "We must always consider the person. Here we enter into the mystery of the human being. In life, God accompanies persons, and we must accompany them, starting from their situation." Furthermore, the pope's image of the church as a field hospital fits with what Christ achieves through us in these celebrations of his amazing grace. "The thing the church needs most today is the ability to heal wounds and to warm the hearts of the faithful; it needs nearness, proximity. I see the church as a field hospital after battle. It is useless to ask a seriously injured person if he has high cholesterol and about the level of his blood sugars! You have to heal his wounds. Then we can talk about everything else. Heal the wounds, heal the wounds…. And you have to start from the ground up."[1]

It has been my repeated experience that when the sacraments are celebrated well and generously, with care and love, they offer healing and peace to those whose battles in life now leave them bruised and laid low; and to others joy, strength, and courage to reenter the fray.

Let's now boldly explore these seven special gifts given to us by Christ in such a way that these symbols and signs will not only change us but have the power to transform the world.

I

Baptism

AT A BAPTISM I did last year, an older Catholic couple complained to me that the invitation had been to a "christening." "We don't do christenings in the Catholic Church, Father," they confidently asserted, "we do baptisms." I asked them what they thought the difference was. "One's Protestant, the other's Catholic." While that may be somewhat true in usage, it's wrong in fact. "Do you know what the word *baptism* means?" I asked. They didn't have a clue. They just knew it was Catholic.

To *christen* is literarily to make someone a Christian, which is precisely what we do in the sacrament of baptism. The Greek word *baptizo* means to "to wash" or "to immerse." Like Jesus, who went down into the waters of the Jordan, the earliest Christians fully immersed adults and children in the baptismal pool. Although "sprinkling" with water over the head at the baptismal font became common for centuries, today the more ancient practice of full immersion of adults and children is strongly encouraged. More on this later.

Who Can Be Baptized?

Of all the times that my concerned Catholic couple could have invoked a Catholic/Protestant distinction, a baptismal ceremony was the least appropriate moment. Baptism is our most important sacrament. Without it we don't get to any other sacrament. It is also our most ecumenical sacrament, which is why the Protestant versus Catholic distinction is wrong. If ever a Catholic, Orthodox, Anglican, Lutheran, Presbyterian, Methodist, or Congregationalist wants to move into another of those Christian families, they should never be rebaptized. Even in the worst days of sectarianism, the Catholic Church never rebaptized a person who could prove that they were baptized in another mainstream Christian denomination, because it's one Christ, one faith, and one baptism.

That's true except for the Baptists because they don't hold to infant baptism. They dedicate children and argue that baptism should be an adult decision. Most Pentecostal Christians often rebaptize because they argue that only a full immersion baptism is valid. It's strange that groups who want to be so biblically literal about the amount of water used at Jesus's baptism are not literal regarding the place of the water—the River Jordan. So, volume matters; geography doesn't.

Baptisms are the happiest of liturgies at which I preside. As Clare Watkins rightly observes, "Baptism is the small event which is the beginning of the great drama of salvation."[1] However, sometimes I am the second minister the parents come to see about doing the ceremony. The first deacon or priest has given the parents a grilling: "Are you going to return to the practice of the faith? Are you going to become registered and a paid-up member of the parish? Will you be sending the child to a Catholic school?" Some parents are even told that they cannot have their baby baptized unless they attend the parish's baptismal course or preparation evening.

While I believe in good preparation for each and every sacrament, baptism included, and have no problem in providing engaging sessions for adult faith formation, it is wrong and often pastorally dangerous for any priest or parish to make the practice of the faith, parish registration, sending the child to a Catholic school, or attending a baptismal course a *precondition* for celebrating the sacrament. Some parents cannot articulate why they want to have their baby baptized. They are sincere in wanting to do their best in raising the child a Catholic, or they have a vague sense that it is a good idea, or they are doing it because Nana said they had to. While we should invite parents and adults to deepen their faith, we can never use a sacrament as a tool of coercion: "If you do not respond to the faith in the way we think you should, then you cannot get your child baptized." This position is even against canon law.

Canon 868 states that the only grounds a baptism can be denied is where there is no hope that a child will be brought up in the Catholic religion. And even then, canon law says the baptism is not to be refused but is to be "delayed" until such hope might be established. Baptism should never be used as an opportunity to get to the parents. It is always about what Christ is doing and how he is welcoming the child into the community of the church. It is a brave priest or deacon who decides who should and shouldn't be baptized based simply on whether the parents will line up for evangelization sessions. Pope Francis has spoken out forcefully on this subject, emphatically telling a group of newly ordained priests, "It is never necessary to refuse baptism to someone who asks for it!" Where I might suggest delaying the sacrament would be the scandalous situation where the parents have told me and their family and friends that they have absolutely no desire to raise the child in the faith in any way, shape, or form, and that the ceremony is only for show. I have never encountered this and hope not to.

Sometimes it is claimed that parents are "only having their child baptized to get them into the Catholic grade school," to which I reply, "And the downside is?" Last time I checked, we believe that baptism is a good thing, and many regard a Catholic education as a good thing too. So, even conceding the parent's mixed motivations—it is rare to find many motivations that are completely pure—their decision to baptize leads to two very good outcomes.

Don't tell some deacons and priests, but they do not own the sacraments. Christ does. This is rock solid Catholic sacramental theology. Christ baptizes, marries, confirms, forgives, ordains, anoints, and hosts us all at the Eucharist. I may be administering the sacrament in Christ's name, but Christ is the actor. Don't get me wrong; I believe in the good order of sacraments. I am not liturgically cavalier, but once we take seriously that it is Christ who performs each and every sacrament, through the minister, we can let go and let God.

It is good to recall that when the Lord, in whose life we are baptized, was on earth, he called people on the religious fringe to himself. Why then would we be surprised he is still doing it today? Sometimes we need to get out of the way and let the Holy Spirit do his or her thing. The old rule holds here: "It doesn't matter where you start. It matters where Christ will finish it."

Earliest Christianity knew all about the truth of that rule. For hundreds of years, all one needed for baptism was to profess faith in Jesus Christ. Catechetical instruction was always after the baptism in the *mystagogia* (Greek for "mystery") period where one learned the demands of the profession that he or she had made, the mysteries in which we believe, and how to live *the way* as the faith was called. They knew that the rite of baptism is itself a teacher. That's why if anyone approaches us in good faith and requests a baptism, and they say yes to the question, "Do you fully understand the serious responsibility you are undertaking?" we have to trust that they will live that out according to their lights: "May God who has begun this good work in you, bring it to completion." In other words, even the desire to be baptized is the action of amazing grace—even if it is not expressed the way we may want.

When I was a newly ordained deacon, I was sent to St. Canice's parish in Kings Cross, the red-light district of Sydney. Within weeks of arriving, I was approached after Mass one Sunday by a same-sex couple who wanted to have their twins baptized. This couple's daughters were conceived via IVF with sperm donated by a good friend of their mothers. The twins were already booked into a Catholic daycare center and grade school. We never covered a case like this in my seminary education, so I sought advice from my seventy-one-year-old Irish, Jesuit pastor. He was well known to be both theologically conservative and pastorally sensitive. After detailing my case, he looked at me and said, "What's the actual problem?" "Well," I ventured, "the process of conception and the lifestyle of the couple are at variance with the Church's teaching." "Did they teach you nothing in the seminary?" he countered. "Those beautiful girls, who are made in the image and likeness of God, in whatever way they came to be created, are the ones invited by Christ

4

to faith in him, and they are, strictly, the ones making the request of the Church. If you don't baptize them, I will—happily." It was the first of many important theological lessons I learned from him.

Once we go down the road of refusing sacraments on the grounds of the visible outcomes we want to see, where do we stop and who decides? What about the person who keeps confessing the same sin each time they come to confession? Do I judge them not to be serious about his or her purpose of amendment? What about a person who attends daily Mass, and whom I know to be a terrible gossip before and after Mass—sometimes even in the church? Do I refuse holy communion on the basis that it would appear the sacrament is having no appreciable impact on his/her charity? What criteria should we put around confirmation? How much assurance do I need that a couple to be married in the church will have a lifelong, monogamous, and loving marriage? I take them at their word. Could I exclude a man from the deaconate or priesthood who minsters in Christ's name but seemingly cares nothing for the poor, and only wants to deal with already committed Catholics? Should I withhold anointing someone who has no expectation that this sacrament will heal them?

I live by the line, "I baptize anyone that moves. I marry anyone that moves. And I bury anyone that doesn't."

Who Can Baptize?

Because some young parents delay the baptism of their children, we sometimes have very anxious grandparents. Many of them were taught that, if an unbaptized child dies, they go to limbo (Latin for "edge" or "boundary"). It remains a theological opinion that argues that baptism is so essential for entry into heaven that even unbaptized babies, who are unable to commit serious sin knowingly, freely, and deliberately, cannot be admitted because they have not been freed from original sin. Theologians who held this opinion even came to consider this was a bit tough, so they posited that there must be another place or state, on the boundary of heaven, where unbaptized babies were eternally happy but never saw God face-to-face. Limbo was born. It was never official Catholic doctrine, but it made its way into the teaching and preaching of the church.

In 2007, the International Theological Commission published "The Hope of Salvation for Infants Who Die without Being Baptized" and concluded that there are "strong grounds for hope that God will save infants when we have not been able to do for them what we would have wished to do, namely, to baptize them into the faith and life of the Church." That same year, Pope Benedict authorized its publication, adding that this conclusion was consistent with the church's teaching. Limbo was now officially sidelined.

Even if many grandparents know of these relatively recent developments regarding limbo, the teaching they received as children trumps everything. This obligation to race babies to the font leads to some comical situations. On more than one occasion, after I have performed their grandchild's baptism, the grandmother will say, "Well, Father, thank God the baptism has been done. Jack and I were starting to think it would never happen. Mind you, we did a little ceremony a couple of years ago." My sacramental antenna goes up. "Mary and Jack, tell me about your ceremony." "When she was eighteen months old, we were looking after Sarah for the weekend. At bath time on the Saturday night, I said to Harry 'They aren't going to baptize this child so let's do the deed.' I got a cup of water and poured it over her head three times, didn't I Harry?" Harry approvingly nods. "It wasn't anything official, but it made us feel better." "May I ask you a few more questions?" "Ask away," says Mary. "Did you intend to baptize Sarah or were you joking around? Did you use water? Did you invoke the Father, Son, and Holy Spirit as you poured it? Were you there as a witness, Jack?" They positively reply to each of these inquiries.

"Well," I discretely tell them, "I am pleased you did not tell me this before today's ceremony because, strictly, I could not have done it. What you did two years ago was a full and true baptism. Today, all I should have done was enroll her name into the baptismal register, knowing that it might have started World War III in your family." Mary and Jack are shocked.

It is one of the surprising gifts of baptism that, while it is the most important sacrament we celebrate, it does not need a deacon, priest, or bishop to perform it. Any validly baptized person can baptize another person provided they have the right intention—they are serious about what they are doing—they use water, they invoke the Trinity, and there is a witness to the ritual.

It is more usual and more appropriate, however, for a minister of the church to baptize a child or an adult, because this event is not about one's family as much as it is about the wider family of the church. That's why it is always preferable for baptisms to occur in the parish church because it connects one's own family to the whole Christian community in the place where they generally gather to pray. Of course, this never applies when necessity dictates otherwise.

Why Should We Bother with Baptism?

The church believes that children and adults have a spiritual life, or a soul, that needs as much care and nurture as their body, mind, and emotions. First, baptism recognizes that all of us are more than we can see and touch, that we have a creative and loving spirit that equally defines who we are, and that this spiritual life within us shares in God and is God in us. We don't have to use any imagination to look in the face of our infants and children to recognize that something greater than we can see and touch is going on. If we recognize this spiritual dimension in our lives, then we want to nurture it.

Some people argue that it's better to wait for a child to reach maturity before deciding about baptism. If we recognize that our children have a spiritual reality, we want to care for it from the beginning. In terms of nutrition, education, ethical training, emotional care, and physical activity, we don't wait until they are eighteen to see if they want to eat vegetables, go to school, learn what they think is right or wrong, be loved, or do exercise. Even though our children might adapt, change, or even reject the earlier choices we have made for them in these regards, we know, instinctively, that in terms of their body, emotions, and mind, we must make the best choices we can for their development from the start. Baptism has provided the best start to many people's spiritual development for over two thousand years.

Some people grow up to adapt, change, or reject the religious choice their parents have made for them earlier in life. That's their right. Others have found that even though they may not practice their Christian faith all that much, it provides them with a personal foundation and an ethical road map upon which they make decisions for their lives. And even though some parents are very sincere about leaving the decision about religion until later, "later" rarely comes. I have yet to meet the parents who deferred all religious choosing for their children so "they can choose for themselves later" and then set about exposing their children to the varieties of Christianity and then Buddhism, Judaism, Islam, and Hinduism just for starters. Some adults remain unbaptized, knowing nothing about the range of choices from which they were supposed to have chosen.

Is Baptism a Form of Brainwashing?

Some people say that baptism is the beginning of Christian brainwashing. If that's true, it seems, these days, that we are the worst brainwashers in the world, as many young adults don't seem to have any trouble walking away from Christianity if they feel it is not answering their needs at that time. One of the privileges of their ability to do this is that they can always choose to return to the church when they have need of our care and support—when they get married, when they need to bury their loved ones who have died, or when they want to have their own children baptized. Even if baptism is only about initiating our children into a Christian community within which they can come for "hatching, matching, and dispatching" then it is a real service to give them such a community that can come to mean so much more than this as well.

What we are doing at baptism is welcoming children into the people of God, who believe in the saving love of Jesus Christ expressed in a family of his disciples around the world that provides them with a sense of belonging and has an ancient tradition of saints and sinners who have found within Christian faith a purpose, direction, and meaning for their lives. It helps people deal with the ups and downs of their daily living, to hold onto hope in this world, and to keep one eye on the life to come after we die.

The Liturgy of Baptism

Let's consider the liturgy of baptism, not only because it is our most important sacrament, but because it is instructive about the process and formation necessary for every other entry point in the life of grace.

Through Jesus's own baptism by John, we have a share in the dignity of baptism done in his name that also celebrates "here is my son or daughter, and I love them." Though I primarily refer to the baptism of our children, much of what I will say applies to adults as well.

The entire rite of baptism underlines the dignity of the person being initiated into the life of Christ and as a member of the church. In an increasingly hostile world to religion, having and holding faith can be very arduous. We need each other, and we are not meant to be soldiering on alone. There was a good reason why Jesus left behind a community. Trying to do otherwise is to live the "Simon & Garfunkel spirituality" reminiscent of their 1966 song, "I Am a Rock." Good luck living that! It does not seem to be serving our contemporary world well at all.

Christ was never under any illusions about what following him may cost, but he underlines how much we need each other to survive in this world. And we need his protection. We often like to be self-sufficient and bristle when we hear how Christ "protects" us, but that is precisely what he does. And that protection comes through prayer, reading the word, celebrating the sacraments, and participating in the life of the church.

When I do baptisms, I always begin by saying that for the first 250 years of the church's history, this sacrament was celebrated at dawn on the Easter Vigil, not only because the rising sun symbolized Christ's light dawning into our lives, but because baptism was always done in secret. For centuries, Christians who took the waters of baptism at dawn could be dead by lunchtime. For them, baptism was no social day out, or the ritual prelude to a "we've had a baby party," or an elaborate naming ceremony. Baptism was a life-and-death commitment. Standing on the shoulders of the martyrs, most, but not all, Christians now gather for baptism in freedom and peace.

Entering through the Portal

I always start the baptismal ceremony at the back door of the church, since this is the first formal time we will receive this child into the place where the church gathers. For centuries, doors were called portals (from the Latin meaning "entry point" or "gateway")—the word *portal* has had a rebirth recently due to the Internet. Indeed, we know from the earliest descriptions of baptisms that they began outside the church, or in the porch, or in the baptistery—a separate room near the back door of the church or sometimes an entire building opposite the back, west door. The font was situated at the opposite end of the altar, symbolizing our journey from our initiation into Christianity to being in full communion with Christ at the table at the opposite, eastern end.[2]

At the portal of where the community in faith gathers for worship, and using actions and words that extend back to the birth of our faith, and in some instances beyond it, we begin by asking the parents what names they have chosen for their child. I always look up the meaning of these names as it is often a revelation as to the child's personality. Because this baptism connects us to our family faith, it is better if at least one of those names has a Christian history or person behind it. That doesn't mean the names have to be boring. Parents have announced the following names possibly without realizing how Christian they are: Maximus, Apollonia, Polycarp, Bond, Hippo, or Trojan. On occasion, I've had to advise against a few names before the ceremony: Jazzy, Sanity, Yoga, Jealousy, BamBam, Bigboy, Cajun, Drifter, Jedi, and Popeye. What were the parents thinking?

Once the child is called by name, by God and in the church, the parents and sponsors declare that they understand the very serious obligations that, from today on, they will undertake, primarily by being Christian role models for this child. Then, to confirm the declarations just made, the child is claimed for Christ by placing the sign of his cross on his or her forehead before processing to the font.

The Procession to the Font

Before the procession begins, I point out that this ritual journey is not just about getting from point A to point B, but that it begins all the processions this child will make in his or her life into and out of a church for confirmation, Eucharist, penance, marriage, holy orders, and anointing of the sick. It also reminds us of that day when, please God, none of us will be around, when, at a big age and surrounded by his or her great grandchildren, they will recess out of the church, for the final time, in the rite of Christian burial. This short walk starts a lifetime of entries and exits.

After the readings and during the homily, I enjoy telling the godparents the history of their role. Most people like being a godfather or a godmother, but they haven't got a clue where it comes from. The church no longer speaks about godfathers or godmothers. It speaks about sponsors, but that term has not caught on regarding infant baptism. The word *godparents* remains in vogue.

The term *godparents* originates from the time when the earliest Christians could be martyred for the faith. Many of them had left their

Jewish or Gentile families to join the Christian community, so if they were killed for the faith, they did not want their children to return to their non-Christian extended families. In this context, they asked other Christians in God's name to swear that they would take their children into their homes and raise them as their own, becoming their mother or father.

Given this history, it is understandable why asking an atheist, agnostic, or a non-Christian to be a godparent does not make sense. They may be terrific human beings, but essentially, they declare at the ceremony, "I will sponsor you into this Church, and support you in it, but I have never joined it myself, or, I did join it and left years ago!"

Of course, parents can now make whatever arrangements they want regarding legal guardianship, but the role that a godparent can play in a child's life is still, potentially, very special. It is important that they take it seriously. At the very least, I advise godparents never to forget the birthday of their godchild. We should be able to trade in any godparent who forgets our birthday for a new one. I also suggest that it would be good if godparents remember the date of the child's baptism because this is the moment when they entered this child's life in the most special of ways. There is not a day between the time of baptism and the child's eighteenth birthday when the parents can say to a godfather or godmother, "Butt out, it's none of your business!" At baptism, a godchild becomes a godparent's business, and we hope, on behalf of the entire Christian community, they will take their responsibilities very seriously.

Calling on the Saints

After the Liturgy of the Word, we remember that this child has patron saints who are praying with us right now in heaven, and we call on them by name. Our veneration of the saints goes back to the earliest Christians who were killed for their faith. All Saints Day, for example, has its roots in the early church's "Martyrs Day," attested to by a hymn written by St. Ephraim in AD 359. In the seventh century, it became known as All Saints Day.

A saint is someone who the church believes is in heaven with God. When we say that someone has been canonized, we declare that, because of the way they lived their Christian lives, God could not deny them heaven, so they are placed on the list (Latin, the *canon*) of recognized saints. We often think incorrectly that saints are perfect, but, in fact, their greatest witness is how they coped with the difficulties of life, and how they reflected the love of God in a variety of ways.

For most of us, sanctity and martyrdom will not come in dramatic ways. The daily routine of looking after a sick child, spouse, or parent; of living with a mental, physical, emotional, or spiritual illness; the scourge of being unemployed, homeless, or addicted, and the feeling that we are unlovable brings with it the reality of sharing in the lot of the martyrs and saints. At baptism, Roman Catholics, the Orthodox, and High Church Anglicans call on the great multitude of witnesses who went through their own persecutions and found the blessings within their daily lives. They saw God in this world and are now fully alive to him in the next.

Rather than saying the names of several dead people, who most people have never heard of, I research and give a very brief biography of the child's patron saints—who they are and why they were canonized. It brings the Litany of the Saints alive.

Exorcism and Anointing

First, a word about evil. If we believe that one can give oneself to love and good and life, then because we have free will, it must be logically possible for people to give themselves to—choose to embrace— hate, evil, and destruction. It's the only way to explain Hitler, Stalin, and Pol Pot. But in Christian theology, evil is not a more powerful force than good, so one cannot make a greater claim for evil than we make for good in regard to its attractions, effects, and consequences.

At baptisms, as soon as I say the word *exorcism*, half the congregation thinks of a 1973 film, *The Exorcist*. We do not, however, think there is anything evil in this child. In the Prayer of Exorcism, we not only pray that the child be free of the common human condition expressed in and through original sin, but that, like Jesus at his baptism, he or she know an outpouring of God's love. I also hope and pray that this child will grow up to be protected from harm, recognize evil wherever it exists, choose good over evil, and diminish its presence and power in the world. I do not know a parent who, these days, would not pray that their child would not be shielded by and enveloped in the love of God, and that evil would stay far away from them.

I remind the congregation that the anointing before baptism is done with the oil of catechumens (a Greek word meaning "one who is being verbally instructed")—those entering the church—and it is smeared on the breastbone. Early Christians, like all ancient peoples, believed that the heart was the place of love. That idea is with us to this day in the heart-festooned invocation of love on St. Valentine's Day. In this anointing, we pray that the strength of Christ's power may transform this child's heart in love for God, for their neighbor, and for themselves.

At the Font

The place of baptism has changed significantly over the centuries: from the River Jordan to other pools of water, to a walk-in pool set into the floor of the church, to bowls set into simple or elaborate pedestals. Some fonts are seven sided, the perfect number, and some are octagonal, a form between a circle (God) and a square (earth), and so the place where heaven and earth meet. In the early thirteenth century, diocesan decrees emerge requiring the font to have a locked cover so that the holy water could not be stolen for satanic rituals. Eventually it was mandated that fresh water be used each time.[3]

After blessing the water at the font, we profess our common Christian faith. I remind everyone that, in the early church, the commitment to baptism was so serious that just before they baptized, they stopped and asked, "Do you share our beliefs? Do you know what you are doing? Are you sure you wish to proceed?" This has come down to us as our profession of faith, and we proceed to a series of questions to which nearly every mainstream Christian can say yes. My favorite question is the first one: "Do you reject Satan, all his works, and all his empty promises?" I love the idea of evil offering us "empty promises." Perfect! And then we proceed on to profess our ancient and common Christian faith.

The moment of baptism follows, either as a sprinkling or by full immersion, and we pour or immerse three times. While some people understandably think the thrice action of plunging the candidate into the water is about the Trinity, because we say Father, Son, and Holy Spirit as we do it, the number, in fact, symbolizes Christ's three days in the tomb. As we go down into our watery grave three times, we rise to the new life of Easter and are now called to live lives worthy of eternal life.

The first baptism at which I presided was for my niece Emily. I was freshly ordained and a strong advocate for full immersion baptisms. The priest, who happened to be my uncle and my family's local pastor, had recently built a new church with a full immersion font. My mother didn't think it was a great idea. "Why would you distress that child so much with this unnecessary fuss? You always go too far!" she said. That night, while doing some baptismal preparation at my brother and sister-in-law's home, I got the sense they did not think full immersion was necessary either, so I played dirty. "Peter," I said, "you have to know that Mom thinks full immersion is a terrible idea." "Good," he replied, "we'll do it then!"

On the day, at the big moment, I took Emily in my arms and said, "Emily Therese, I baptize you in the name of the Father" and lowered her in and out of the warm water. She thought it was a bath. "And of the Son," repeating the action. She cooed and kicked. "And of the Holy Spirit," but this time, with my confidence up, I went to gently cup some water over her head, which ended being a tsunami in her face. Emily let out a huge scream. My mother jumped up from the first pew, "I told you this was a stupid idea." To which my brother sharply retorted, "Will you please sit down and shut up!"

There are no half measures about immersion. We are in there, boots and all. As Jesus fully immersed himself in our world, so we are fully immersed in Christ. But we're not spared from the world as if we're initiated into a reclusive religious sect. Just as Jesus's baptism was the beginning of his public ministry for which he would pay the ultimate price, so, too, we're sent out to the world knowing that even though we sin, we are loved by a compassionate God and are pleasing to him. We're also sent out to immerse ourselves in the world and discover that because of his baptism, there is not a single place, not even the tomb, where Christ has not gone ahead of us—in the name of the Father, the Son, and Holy Spirit.

Chrismed, Clothed, Enlightened, and Opened

The anointing with chrism is done using the church's holiest oil, chrism (from the Greek word *charisma*: "to anoint"), which is a mixture of olive oil and balsam, so it is the only sweet-smelling oil the church uses. It has wonderful roots in the Old Testament, where chrism was used in coronation ceremonies, the consecration of the Levite priests, and the commissioning of some of the prophets. In using it at baptism, we declare the sacred has now taken up a home within the baptized, who are set aside and strengthened to do God's work in the world. In doing so, we welcome this girl or boy into the royal family of Christ, his school of prophets, and the priesthood of all believers.

It's good to know that the other times the church uses this holiest of oils is at the coronations of kings and queens, ordinations of priests and bishops, at the sacrament of confirmation, and at their dedication of churches where it is smeared on the walls to make the space sacred.

It is best that the parents not bring their children to the ceremony already dressed in their baptismal robe so that, after the actual baptism and the anointing with chrism, and in line with the more ancient custom, we can vest them. The baptismal robe is the external physical sign that they have just spiritually put on the life of Christ. We have these dramatic descriptions of baptisms at the Easter Vigil in the early centuries of Christianity where the candidates came in their work clothes, were smeared with oil, fully immersed in water, and then taken away from the body of the church to soon return in the long white robe of baptism. This is where the *alb* (Latin meaning: "white") that the priest wears at Mass originates. It is not a robe of the ordained; it is the white robe of the common priesthood of all Christ's faithful. Anyone who has been baptized could wear their alb, or baptismal robe, to Mass.

We then present the parents and godparents with the Light of Christ, for this child has been "enlightened by Christ" and is "always to walk as a child of the Light." Usually, we get to keep our baptismal candles after the ceremony. We should. It would be wonderful to think it might be lit again at the other sacraments of initiation: Eucharist and confirmation. It also makes sense for that candle to be a light at their marriage or ordination ceremonies, and finally, in the rite of burial, as we wait to go out to meet the Lord "with all the saints in the heavenly kingdom," we might clutch our baptismal candle in our casket before we are buried or cremated.

Finally, we pray the *Ephphatha* prayer (a Hebrew word meaning "to be open") over the child. Here, we invoke Jesus's actions in Mark 7:34, where he comes across the deaf and mute man and places his hands on his ears, touches his tongue, and prays, "ephphatha," and the man can immediately hear and speak. We pray that Christ will soon touch and open the child's eyes and ears to read and hear God's Word and their mouth to proclaim it to the glory of God.

The reason we have such an elaborate ritual is because of the baptism of the Lord. In it, and like the other-Christ we are now meant to be, we discover that our true identity is in God, that we are beloved by him, and, through Christ, we have become members of God's family, his sons and daughters. What is a more appropriate way of welcoming anyone into this world than having a community of frail, human believers initiate its members by reminding them that original sin does not have the last word; original grace does? For those of us baptized in Christ, the Father's love and mercy always and everywhere have the final say on everything and everyone.

Every day following our baptism, the task is to keep claiming our Christian dignity through the ways we choose to spend our lives, and to change our world for the better because of the love lavishly announced about us and to us at our baptism. It is the great sacrament of hope.

"I hope!"

Arguably one of the most vivid secular explorations of being baptized and living it came in the 1994 smash hit film *The Shawshank Redemption*. In 1947, Andy Dufresne is wrongfully convicted of his wife's murder and sentenced to life in prison at Shawshank Penitentiary, which is run by the God-fearing Warden Norton. In time, Andy is befriended by a fellow lifer, Red, the great "fixer" of the jail. In 1966, Norton discovers that Andy is actually innocent of murder. The warden has the informant killed to keep Andy in jail. Andy plots his escape and tells Red that if he ever gets probation, he can meet him on the beach in Mexico. "Remember, Red, hope is a good thing, maybe the best of things. And no good thing ever dies."

For years Andy builds a tunnel to the sewer through which he crawls to make his bid to freedom. "Andy Dufresne—who crawled through a river of shit and came out clean on the other side." On a rain-drenched night, he reaches the other side. Red eventually gets out and follows Andy's instructions until he makes his bid for freedom on the other side of the border. "There's a harsh truth to face. No way I'm going to make it on the outside. All I do anymore is think of ways to break my parole, so maybe they'd send me back. Terrible thing, to live in fear. All I want is to be back where things make sense. Where I won't have to be afraid all the time. Only one thing stops me. A promise I made to Andy."

Now, deciding to break loose of the history and personal chains that keep him locked up in the cell of his own heart and mind, he crosses the physical, spiritual, and emotional border. "I think it's the excitement only a free man can feel, a free man at the start of a long journey whose conclusion is uncertain. I hope I can make it across the border....I hope to see my friend and shake his hand. I hope the Pacific is as blue as it has been in my dreams. I hope."

The word *redemption* literarily means "buying back." It comes from the practice in the ancient world where there were two types of slaves—those who were born or forced into slavery, usually for life, and those who paid off a debt or a crime by becoming a slave, usually for a period. The second type of slaves could be set free when someone else paid their debts or the ransom their master now demanded for them was settled. They would then be either the slave of the purchaser or set free completely.

St. Paul introduced this metaphor into Christian theology to describe how we, who are enslaved by our destructive behavior, gained a liberator in Christ who entered into a sinful world and subjected himself to its violence and death in order to set us free. At its best, the notion of Christ the Redeemer shows us that we do not have to live destructively anymore. Now claimed by the love of Christ, we are no longer slaves, but his friends. Indeed, through the redeeming work of Christ, we have been welcomed into God's family and shown the path to life.

The parallels between Andy's redemption of the everyman and guilty Red and Christ's actions toward us in baptism are striking. In the film, the jail is where we are enslaved by and to our most destructive behavior. In such a place, an innocent man is the first to break out of the impregnable fortress and points the way to freedom and new life. Red does not need to crawl through a river of shit because Andy has already done that and thereby shows the way to the freedom beyond. Andy has spoken and written his words, a testament, that needs knowing interpretation about how to find the keys that unlock the path to new life. But Red then needs the courage to start on the journey. Red knows where to find Andy because Andy has prepared the place for him, has gone ahead of him, and waits for him there. Red goes to the tree of knowledge (Gen 2:16–17) and there it becomes the tree of life (Rev 22:2). Red meets Andy on the beach (John 21) where the Pacific is as blue as Andy promised, and they can "get busy living" rather than "get busy dying."

Baptism is the great sacrament of a hope that leads to freedom and new life.

2

Eucharist

Broken and Poured Out

IN THE NEW TESTAMENT, we have two comple-
mentary traditions about the institution of the Eucharist: the meal
itself and the mission of love and service to which it leads. Writing from
Ephesus (ca. AD 53–57), St. Paul gives us the most ancient description
of what he learned about the Lord at the Last Supper:

> For I received from the Lord what I also handed on to you,
> that the Lord Jesus on the night when he was betrayed took
> a loaf of bread, and when he had given thanks, he broke it
> and said, "This is my body that is for you. Do this in remem-
> brance of me." In the same way he took the cup also, after
> supper, saying, "This cup is the new covenant in my blood.
> Do this, as often as you drink it, in remembrance of me." For
> as often as you eat this bread and drink the cup, you pro-
> claim the Lord's death until he comes. (1 Cor 11:23–26)

In Mark (written for Rome ca. 70), Matthew (written possibly
from Antioch, ca. mid-eighties), and Luke (ca. mid-eighties), we are
told the following: an unnamed woman in Simon's house anoints Jesus
before the Last Supper as a recognition of his impending death; Judas

strikes a deal with the priests for money to hand over the Lord; Jesus then prepares and celebrates the Passover with his disciples; and during this meal he predicts that one of his closest friends will betray him. Mark and Matthew then say Jesus takes bread and wine, while Luke says he takes wine and then the bread and speaks of giving them himself. He then predicts that Peter will deny him that very night. He goes to the Garden of Gethsemane on the Mount of Olives where Judas arrives with an armed crowd and betrays Jesus with a kiss.

For St. Paul and the first three Gospels, the focus of the Last Supper is in the action of the meal: breaking apart the bread; pouring out the cup of wine; and these being shared. These rituals became so identifiable with what they described, that the earliest name the Christians gave to the Eucharist was "the breaking of the bread" (see Acts 2:42).

Every time I reflect on the Last Supper in Paul, Matthew, Mark, and Luke, I think of that well-known African-American soul song: "Let us break bread…drink wine…love one another…(and) praise God together on our knees." These verses finish with the line: "When I fall on my knees with my face to the rising Son, O Lord, have mercy on me." By celebrating the Eucharist, we pray that Christ will continue to "Easter in us" and that there is no service too small, no act of kindness too insignificant, and no moment of love inconsequential in our service of all God's people. We look for opportunities to take up the commission to serve all those who feel spent with the brokenness of their lives. And when we do this, we discover it has an extraordinary effect on us. With our brothers and sisters whom we serve, we can recognize the face of the rising Son and praise God together on our knees.

John Gets Down and Dirty

The idea of getting on our knees is even more explicitly played out in the Fourth Gospel. Though John, writing from Ephesus (ca. 100), adds his own details to the story of the day of the Last Supper as Mark, Matthew, and Luke outlined it, the dramatic difference is that, while

John writes that Jesus gathers his disciples at the Passover, he records nothing of the action of Jesus at the meal but focuses on what happened after it was over. John is the only Gospel to tell us how Jesus got up from the table and washed the feet of his disciples.

While the washing of a guest's feet was a custom in Jesus's day, a Jewish host certainly never did it. Indeed, not even Jewish servants usually performed this act. If possible, it was the task of the least in the house, one for the Gentile, or non-Jewish, servant. No wonder Peter objects to it so strongly. The household codes also tell us that it was not done regularly, but only on those occasions where guests who had completed a long trip were received into the home at journey's end.

By doing this act, Jesus announces the end of the road for weary travelers. For him and his disciples, the journey they had embarked upon years before was now about to take a final turn. Indeed, it was to be a definitive rite of passage. And in doing so, Jesus also demonstrated what he had preached, that anyone who wants to be first must be last of all and servant of all. In this ritual action, he walks the talk and does the job of the most-lowly slave in the house.

Because dusty, weatherworn feet were objectionable in Jesus's day, I like to think his action at the Last Supper also reveals that, as Christ welcomes us to his table, he also says there is not a part of any of us that is untouchable or shameful, that nothing is beyond God's loving touch—not one part—and that our God, revealed in Jesus, "gets down and gets dirty" so that, following his lead, we can rise up to claim our dignity as his disciples and commit ourselves again to acts of loving service that set other people free. "So if I, your Lord and Teacher, have washed your feet, you also ought to wash one another's feet" (John 13:14).

We Walk across the Sea

John Francis Collins summarizes the six biblical elements that come together in what Jesus did at the Last Supper:

The Passover, when the Hebrews captive in Egypt marked the doorposts of their homes with the blood of a lamb; upon seeing this sign, the spirit of the Lord passed over these homes, saving them from a terrible plague (Exodus 12:21–28);

the Exodus of the Hebrews from slavery in Egypt and the food (manna) provided by God in the desert (Exodus 16);

meals that Jesus shared with the outcasts of society (Mark 14:3–9);

his death on the cross (Mark 15:21–40);

his rising from the dead (John 20, 21);

the image of the eternal banquet where he will preside when he brings creation to completion at the end of time (Luke 14:15–24).[1]

In our celebration of the Eucharist, we are familiar with claiming the last four events, which we will return to later, but the first two themes can sometimes be underexplored in Christian theology, despite our reading about the Passover on Holy Thursday. For Christians, the freedom gained by the chosen people in Egypt was definitively consummated in the freedom embodied in the life, death, and resurrection of Jesus.

In a profound poem, French Jesuit Didier Rimaud makes a stark connection between our celebration of the Eucharist and our liberation begun in the story of the Exodus:

In remembrance of you,
We take the bread of Easter in our hands,
This bread do we consume:
It does no longer taste of bitter herbs, nor of unleavened bread.
It is the bread of a land promised us where we shall be set free.

In remembrance of you,
We take the wine of Easter at our feast,
This wine do we hold dear:

It does no longer taste of bitter springs, nor of dark salty pools.
It is the wine of a land promised us where we shall be made whole.

> In remembrance of you,
> From exile we return!
> In remembrance of you,
> We walk across the sea![2]

The Passover and resulting exodus event are the defining moments in the history of Israel. However, for Christians, they can be distant events that happened to "the Jews," and of little consequence for us today. For two reasons, however, the exodus should be a defining moment in our lives too. First, as Christians, we look to Jesus for salvation. His personal and religious identity was inextricably and proudly tied to the Passover and the exodus. This is one of the reasons why it is patently absurd for a Christian to be anti-Semitic. Such Christians end up hating the very religious tradition that formed Jesus, his mother, and St. Joseph, as well as the twelve apostles. If God chose our Jewish brothers and sisters as the people from whom the Lord would come, who are we to declare him mistaken? One of the worst things Christianity has done to the memory of Jesus is to strip him of his religious heritage. This has terrible consequences. If we are sincere about getting to know the historical Jesus, it helps to have some devout Jewish friends to guide us. The church is actively mindful of this heritage when at the prayers of offering during the Preparation of the Gifts the priest says, "Blessed are you, Lord God of all creation," which is taken from the Passover seder.

Second, the Passover and Exodus are now metaphors for what God is doing for all of us in Christ. Many of us know what it is like to be stuck. Imprisoned by our body, mind, or soul, these places can be very dark. The first Passover in Egypt and the Last Supper, upon which it is based, were celebrated in the most desolate of circumstances: the Israelites were in exile and enslaved, and Jesus was on the eve of his passion and death; the Israelites held on to the hope that they would be freed, and Jesus had complete trust that the Father would remain faithful; the hope of the Israelites led to the Exodus, and for Jesus, his hope led to the resurrection. But there is one dramatic and crucial difference between the Passover and the Last Supper. The Israelite's freedom, which is a murderous story, cost many lives in Egypt—the firstborn son of every Egyptian family. By contrast, not one life was directly or completely lost in the wake of the resurrection, not even Jesus, who is ultimately raised from the dead. In fact, Jesus's death and resurrection gave all people the opportunity to know eternal life. God was so despairing of human death and the never-ending cycle of violence that Jesus went to his death so that death would be no more.

The Last Supper gives us "food for the journey" so that we can return from our exile and walk across the sea, even as we taste the bitter herbs and the dark, salty pools of the world's injustice. The service and hospitality of the Eucharist establish the pattern of our daily lives, remembering that by journey's end we will, in Christ, inherit the land promised us, where all creation will be made whole and we will be set free.

Food for the Journey

Of all the other allegorical narratives about the Eucharist in the Gospels—the feeding of the multitudes, the wedding feast at Cana, and the other wedding banquets—the most important is in Luke's Gospel, where Jesus meets the disciples on the road from Jerusalem to Emmaus. With good reason, this story is the best parallel we have in the New Testament to our weekly celebration of the Eucharist, connecting us to the church's earliest experiences of the Eucharist. Luke reminds his community that, even though they—like us—are prevented from seeing Jesus, they can still have a life-changing encounter with him, an experience of his presence.

The setting of the story is important. Cleopas and his unnamed companion (possibly a woman disciple) are leaving Jerusalem brokenhearted that the one in whom they hoped, Jesus of Nazareth, has been executed. Even though there were tales of him rising, they were despondent as they returned to their former lives. It is precisely into this place of hopelessness, amid their pain and suffering, that they meet the risen Christ—where they are, as they are.

As they accompany each other, Christ listens to their expectations, hopes, and disappointments, and only after they have expressed the reality of their situation does Christ open the Scriptures to them. In doing so, he takes their disillusionment and enables them to see the connections with the story of salvation. This leads them to hope. Even then, they do not recognize Jesus until he breaks the bread, and in that action, he is revealed as the one in whom they had been hoping. This experience sends them back to Jerusalem to witness to the power of Christ's resurrection.

Note the verbs used to describe the action in the Emmaus story. Christ *walks, inquires, explains, interprets, hosts, breaks, shares, reveals,* and in turn, *commissions.* This can happen to us at every Eucharist where, as part of our journey of faith, we embark on our road to Emmaus.

There is never any point in us pretending before God to be any different. God sees our heart and mind and wants to meet us amid our life, whatever it may be like. The Emmaus story teaches us that Jesus first wants to listen to us before he wants us to listen to him. Emmaus, however, was not just about the disciples and their lives, in the same way that the Eucharist is not just about our lives either. Christ opens the Scriptures to us each week so that we can make sense of our experience, see the ways in which God is present and absent, and recognize our own foolishness. As with the Emmaus disciples, we are welcomed to the table of the Lord where he hosts us and breaks the bread, and, thereby, we recognize the gift and giver. This meal enables us to go out and proclaim to all we meet that Christ is risen. And I have always liked the way Cleopas and his girlfriend describe their encounter on the road as though their hearts were burning within them. Religious experience matters, for it is the moment when ideas become encounters, and for Christians, when a proposal becomes a person.

Similarly, we come to know forgiveness, beauty, and conscience through experience, so too, some of us have been privileged to know the reality of God because we have encountered God's love. Indeed, for Christians, religious experience is pivotal to our faith. Rather than speak about this in the abstract, let me share my own experience.

Coming from a very devout Irish Catholic, Australian family, growing up, my life revolved around my large extended and smaller immediate family, as well as the local Catholic Church. I went to Catholic elementary, intermediate, and high schools. My uncle was a priest and many relatives were religious. Despite my education extending through the rebellious 1970s, I never questioned God or the prerogatives of the church. I was a proud Catholic, but my relationship was primarily to the tribe—the church—not to God. At the age of fifteen, this was soon to change. The day was toward the end of 1978, when five young Catholics—Peter, Judy, Maree, Vince, and Peter—walked into my high school religious education class. All were older than me, between eighteen and twenty-two, and I knew some of them. As soon as they started speaking, I was captivated. They began by saying that they had sat where we were sitting. They identified with us as being ordinary young Catholics searching for meaning and purpose. And then they told us how they went on a retreat that changed their lives. It had been put together by a man who was to become a mentor and friend, Fr. Ray O'Leary. The entire retreat was based on the pivotal question in Mark's Gospel: "Who do you say that I am?"

The five young evangelists in my classroom consequently reported having a deep encounter with God and an experience of their faith in Christ. I had never heard any Catholic—let alone a young adult—talk like this. Not only was their faith unashamedly public, they were palpably, infectiously happy. I knew these people. I could not dismiss them as Jesus freaks or screwballs. They lived up the street from me, and indeed, two of the four men had sat in the room where we were sitting only five years earlier. They were happy. I remember thinking that I had never seen any demonstrably happy Catholics talk about their faith like this. I was hooked.

While making this retreat, we were challenged about our faith, about Christ. We were reassured that God is loving, forgiving, and merciful. It was like I was hearing this for the first time, and it gave me hope and confidence.

There were extended periods of silence and wonderful prayer sessions, and just like the disciples at Emmaus, the weekend culminated in a long and life-changing celebration of the Eucharist after which we were asked if we chose Christ or not. We had a very discreet and Catholic version of an altar call, where, if we chose to step out in faith, we were prayed over. There was no pressure. We were explicitly told that we were free to say yes or no, but in saying yes, along with scores of others, I had a religious experience, a flooding of the heart. In fact, I would not be writing this book if it were not for that retreat.

Somewhere in having a religious experience, I went from being a member of the tribe to understanding why the tribe exists. I had an encounter with the presence of God. My heart burned within me and it's still glowing. And just like the disciples, this encounter is not just for me, for us, but it impels all of us to mission.

Called and Sent

Archbishop Fulton Sheen was rightly fond of saying, "It's the Mass that matters." Catholics use "Mass" most of the time to describe the Eucharist, but many do not know what it means. The word *Mass* comes from the moment when the priest sent the congregation forth with these Latin words: "*Ite, missa est.*" The word *missa*, which, in the ancient world, meant "to be dismissed," has taken on a new meaning in the liturgy. In 2007, Pope Benedict XVI observed that "in Christian usage it [*missa*] gradually took on a deeper meaning. The word 'dismissal' has come to imply a 'mission.' These few words [*Ite, missa est*] succinctly express the missionary nature of the Church" (*Sacramentum Caritatis* 51).

When we are going to Mass, we are saying we are going to our commissioning to live what we have just professed, and that's why some element of social justice should feature in our liturgy—especially through preaching, the prayers of the faithful, and even the bulletin—so that we may learn how we can apply what we just heard in our daily lives.

This approach to the Eucharist is very traditional. St. Augustine (354–430) famously commented in a sermon,

> What you see…is bread and a cup. This is what your eyes report to you. But your faith has need to be taught that the bread is the body of Christ, the cup the blood of Christ.… "How is the bread his body? And the cup, or what is in the cup, how is that his blood?" That which is seen has physical appearance; that which is understood has spiritual fruit. If, then, you wish to understand the body of Christ, listen to the Apostle as he says to the faithful, "You are the body of Christ, and His members" (1 Cor. 12:27). If, therefore, you are the body of Christ and His members, your mystery has been placed on the Lord's table, you receive your mystery. You reply "Amen" to that which you are, and by replying you consent. For you hear "The Body of Christ," and you reply "Amen." Be a member of the body of Christ so that your "Amen" may be true….If we receive the Eucharist worthily, we become what we receive. (Easter Sermon, no. 272)

It's not, therefore, just the static presence of Christ we behold, but also the challenge to enter his activity of sacrificial love. Every time we step forward and receive communion, we say "Amen" (I affirm) to Jesus Christ as broken and poured out; we reaffirm God's love for us. This is also the intimate moment where God meets us in the most broken parts of our own lives and in those times that we feel completely poured out. God is a companion in our suffering and sacrifices. In turn, it shows us how we should live. Everyone who celebrates the Eucharist is also saying they are prepared to pay the price of being one with him in being broken and poured out in love for the world.

This theology counters a magical understanding of the Eucharist where divine incantations are said over terrible people who are mystically turned into good people instead. Dr. Billy Graham once said, "Going to church no more *makes* you a Christian, than living in a garage would *make* you a car." While Dr. Graham and I both think that going to church matters, it is what we do away from the Eucharist that proves it is having an impact for the better. Gerard Goldman summarizes it well:

> Our liturgical life needs to reflect the 'coming in' and 'going out' movement of Mission. It is important that the Church emphasizes that Eucharist is not an end in itself; that we never lose sight that Eucharist serves Mission....To be sure, the Eucharist will always be the centerpiece of our liturgical and community life, but it is the centerpiece only because it feeds us for God's mission.[3]

There are two other words we use for the Mass: *eucharist* and *liturgy*. The Greek word *eukharistos* means "grateful," "to be thankful." This encapsulates, of course, our thanksgiving to God for the life, death, and resurrection of Christ and that his way, truth, and life see his joy complete in us and offer us eternal life. Indeed, we have much for which to be very thankful.

In my work with teachers, one of the things that has struck me in recent years is how many of them say, "The two fastest disappearing words in the English language are 'please' and 'thank you' because these days kids think everything is a right." We should not just blame parents and their children alone for this. Have you noticed that common courtesy is waning, and how some adults seem to be demanding of everyone around them? It is often embarrassing how some people speak to those who are serving us. Good customer service should not come because I yell louder than everyone else. We are better than that!

In fact, we need to cultivate a habit of saying "please" and "thank you," not just because it is a sign of a civil society, but because it enables us to recognize the dignity of each person who deserves our respect, even if they are being paid to do their job. It helps create a world in which people are never mistaken for commodities.

If we are going to celebrate the Eucharist worthily, it starts long before we arrive at church. It starts at the family dining table. As a priest, I often have the honor of being invited into people's homes for a family meal. It's almost always a very enjoyable experience. Mind you, things have changed in many homes, and when I am invited to say a grace before the meal, an assertive adolescent says, "Why are we saying grace? We never say grace! Why are you playing it up for the priest?" I would like to reply, "We're saying grace because sixteen thousand kids your age or younger will die today from starvation. So we take one moment to be grateful for the food we have and the strength it gives us to make the world a more just place for everyone." While I have never actually said that, I really want to!

On one occasion I was invited to a family dinner. This family had been having more than a little trouble with their fourteen-year-old daughter, who was going through a particularly defiant and rebellious stage. The young girl was not happy with the vegetables her mother served at dinner and refused to eat them. The uneaten vegetables became the staging ground for an adolescent conflict. Trying to coax the girl into eating her greens, her mother calmly used some lines I'd heard before: "Wasting food is a sin" and "There are starving people in the world who would be grateful for what you don't want." With that, the girl jumped up and left the dining room. A few minutes later, she returned with an oversized envelope and a marker pen. She began to stuff the food into the envelope asking angrily, "What starving people do you want me to send these vegetables to?" I can honestly say that celibacy never looked better than at that moment.

If the Eucharist is going to be the summit and the source of all our thanksgivings, then it starts with us being grateful for every other meal we receive and share. The late Fr. Pedro Arrupe, the superior general of the Society of Jesus, brings together this gift of gratitude and our mission to change the world when he said, "If there is hunger anywhere in the world, then our celebration of the Eucharist is somehow incomplete everywhere in the world."[4]

The third word we use for the Mass or the Eucharist is *liturgy*, which comes from the Greek word *leitourgia*, which means "the work of the people." In fact, that Greek word comes from *litos* and *ergos*, which literally mean "public" and "service," and that also has special resonance and history for our civil servants. The use of it regarding religious rituals seems to have started with the *Septuagint*, a translation of the Old Testament dating from 3 BCE, where the term was used for the public service of the temple. It's this meaning that crosses into the New Testament and then into the more general Christian usage. These days, liturgy is most often understood as religious ritual.

Clifford Geertz claims that religious ritual is consecrated behavior expressed in dramatic ceremony where the members experience a symbolic fusion of ethos and worldview as they "attain their faith as they portray it."[5] It's not coincidental that the word *ritual* is contained within the word *spirituality*; one without the other is inconceivable.

Whether we use the words *Mass*, *Eucharist*, or *liturgy*, it is essential that our ritual behavior is not about putting on a public show for God. Jesuit priest Frank Wallace wrote a book on prayer that I've never read. I am sure it's a fine book, but I've never got past the front cover and the preface. The title, *Encounter, not Performance*,[6] communicates everything we need to say about the Eucharist. As good as our liturgies should be, it is never about a performance that we think God will enjoy or will make him like us more. In fact, the more we put on a ritual show for God, the more God must wonder why we are going through this routine. God's love is gratuitously and readily available to us. It is a question of claiming that love, so we can live lives worthy of it. At Mass, we are invited by God, and hosted by Christ, to enter a sacred space where the Holy Spirit enables us, through our ritual actions, to encounter and make real the presence of Christ so that we, in turn, become his Body in the world.

A Presence that Is Real

A Protestant friend told me once that he could never contemplate becoming a Roman Catholic "because you are eucharistic cannibals." He was sincere. I was speechless—and that rarely happens. I soon understood what he meant, even if it was provocatively expressed. As Catholics, we must own that, in some popular devotions and pious legends, a link to the physicality of the Eucharist can be too explicit. We are not Christian cannibals, feasting on Jesus's flesh and blood; on his liver, brain, and bones.

The best traditions in the church are careful in the language they use about how Jesus is present in the Eucharist. When the *Catechism of the Catholic Church* speaks of the eucharistic real presence, it never refers to "Jesus," but always to "Christ." This distinction matters. The Eucharist is a sacrament of Easter.

As a Catholic, I believe that Christ, raised by God from the dead, is fully and truly present to me in the consecrated bread and wine at Mass. In 1 Corinthians 15, St. Paul was clear in rebutting two extreme views about the glorified body of Christ: a crude physicalism, where the glorified body of Christ was simply a resuscitation of his corpse; and an overspiritualization, where Christ raised from the dead was an ethereal ghost.

The *Catechism* puts the issue succinctly: "[The] glorious body [is] not limited by space and time but able to be present how and when he wills; for Christ's humanity can no longer be confined to earth" (§645). The risen body and blood of Christ is found in the experience of Easter it signifies—an encounter that transcends the boundaries of human weakness, but at the same time raises it up and heals all the wounds of the body. The divine presence of Christ lives in and through the redeemed physical world, but is not bound or contained by it.

For the first few centuries, Christians adored Christ as they consumed communion. The reservation of the Blessed Sacrament was rare, and then mainly for the sick. From the fifth century, as Christians believed that they were not worthy to receive the Eucharist, their adoration of the risen Lord took the place of communing with him.

Indeed, the Feast of Corpus Christi, the body and blood of Christ, arises in the twelfth century when many Catholics simply never received communion at all but felt close to Christ through the act of adoration. In 1215, the church had to enact a law, which is still in effect today, requiring Catholics to receive communion at least once a year, at Eastertime.

The Second Vatican Council taught that, while the act of adoration is important and consistent with the intensity of our love, receiving the risen Lord in holy communion was the more ancient part of our tradition and a more complete act. Indeed, Vatican II also reminded us that, while we believe that Christ is uniquely and intimately present in the bread of life and the cup of salvation, we also believe that Christ's real presence also comes to us in the word of God, in the gathered assembly of God's people, and in the person of the minister.

Sometimes a few believers can speak of the Eucharist as a magical act. Jesus counters such a notion by telling us that he gives us himself "for the life of the world." There is a significant difference between grace and magic. One is a trick for a show. The other is the power of love, which expresses itself in faith, hope, and service. The Eucharist is not intimate and unique because it is magic. It's not intimate and unique because we only gaze upon the elements. The Eucharist is intimate and unique because ordinary, earthly signs of bread and wine are transformed by God's love and are consumed in faith. As we eat and drink these elements, Christ becomes part of us and we come alive in Christ: blessed, broken, poured out, and shared in love for the life of the world.

Understood in these ways, our belief in the real presence of Christ in the Eucharist moves away from solely celebrating the static presence of Christ in the Blessed Sacrament to the dynamic living out of the real presence in our real lives.

Feasting and Fasting

Babette's Feast (1986) is among one of the finest contemporary parables about the Eucharist. This Oscar-winning film can also be read as an homage to an artist, in this case a culinary artist, but as important as the aesthetical features in the story are, the sacramental reading of it is a much more fascinating one.

Based on Karen Blixen's (writing as Isak Dinesen) novel of the same name, Babette is a Parisian chef who gets caught up in the riots in the French capital in 1871. Her husband and son are killed in the fighting. Babette is helped to escape to a remote village in Norway where a strict Protestant sect takes her in. The founder of the community has died, but his two daughters engage Babette as their cook. The mysterious woman assumes the nature of a servant. They have no idea who she is or what has brought her to their home. In 1885, Babette wins ten thousand francs in a lottery and asks the sisters to let her provide a feast in honor of what would have been the pastor's one hundredth birthday. She spends all her winnings on buying food and wine so that she can provide a banquet for the community who saved her life.

On the night of the meal, the members of the community are anxious about the food and wine they will be served. They have never had such rich fare before and have never tasted alcohol. They decide to eat Babette's feast, but draw no attention to it, offering up their meal as reparation for sin. Present at the feast is a local man who is now a general in the army. While he can't understand how the local villagers can ignore the beauty of the meal, he notes that the only time he has had such a feast was at the Café Anglais from the hands of Paris's most celebrated chef, a woman. Babette remains unseen throughout the dinner, but despite their resistance, her meal has a dramatic effect on the diners. Stories are shared, enmities are resolved, and a new unity celebrated.

Akin to the secrecy of Jesus's identity in Mark's Gospel, Babette's full story is only gradually revealed, and even then, not fully disclosed. Like Mary and Martha of Bethany, the sisters welcome their guest in her need and out of their Christian devotion. Laboring away in hiddenness, Babette comes into her own with the power of the lottery. Then she can plan and execute the anniversary meal, the one she longed to provide for them. She pours all she has into the meal. This last point is worth amplifying. The sisters who've come to rely on her expect that with her newfound fortune Babette will abandon them. Babette remains faithful to them, having become poor and having made her home among the poor. Babette does not give her physical life for a cause, though in many other respects she has died to her old life and been reborn to this one.

The centrality of the meal has extraordinary eucharistic themes. It is called a "feast," one of the metaphors Jesus gave for the kingdom. In fact, the generosity of this feast, where the best of everything is provided for the rich and poor alike, further underlines the metaphor. But it is the effect of this meal that most reveals its nature. There are twelve diners around the table, and most of them do not understand the significance of the meal. Eleven of them fear it as an instrument of the devil. Only one diner, the general, can interpret the signs and fully appreciate the fare placed before him. The meal's effect, however, is indiscriminate— the truth is told, forgiveness is granted, community emerges, and unity is confirmed. The truth telling at the meal is especially allegorical. Following the lead of the Book of Genesis, where Adam and Eve eat of the forbidden fruit of knowledge, the diners share their knowledge and experience of each following the feast's fruit course. Unlike the Genesis story, however, this knowledge does not lead to alienation, but to forgiveness. This is a meal of reconciliation. In a more obscure allusion to Genesis, we are told that by the time Babette hosts the feast, she has been on the island for fourteen years—a time of creation (seven years) and re-creation (seven years).

There are several other Christian symbols throughout the film: the sea, fishing boats, and nets, which evoke thoughts of gospel narratives regarding abundance, discipleship, and the church. Given that the film opens with the singing of a hymn about the new and everlasting Jerusalem, and which remains the film's theme, *Babette's Feast* can be interpreted as a commentary on the eschaton, the end of time.

Windows are especially prominent throughout this film: the sister's neighbor looks at the young soldier as he arrives to court Birgitte, one of the sisters; later, the soldier looks out of his window as he reflects on Birgitte's decision not to marry him; another neighbor sees the sisters come and go, doing the work of their father, "our dearly beloved and departed Pastor"; as Babette eats her simple meal day after day, she looks out of the kitchen window reflecting on the world beyond these shores; one of Babette's regular tasks is to wash and polish the windows of the house; the sisters watch through the windows aghast at the array of exotic goods arriving for the feast. Windows are a cinematic device usually denoting other worlds, but it is not by accident that we call the eyes "the window to the soul." What our eyes behold often forms who we are. What we see through the windows in *Babette's Feast* is regret, grief, and anxiety, as well as the importance of the daily routine. So much of this film revolves around being lost and being found, which is the journey of every soul, and the window here narrates the tale.

In preparation for the feast, there is a delicious clash of cultures between Babette's French Catholicism and the island's Danish Calvinism. Babette is as elaborately sacramental as the villagers are stark and focused on the Word. The result is some of the best ecumenism ever caught on film. The islanders love Babette in her need, as the Word commands, and thereby entertain an angel. Babette transforms their lives through her artistry. Everyone wins. Babette's life is saved, and in turn, she gives life to a rather gray community.

Whether we interpret Babette as an artist, a Christ figure, or a priest, this film narrates how some meals can transform our lives. Christians hold that the eucharistic meal both changes lives, here and now, and prefigures the eternal banquet to come.

One of my professors of liturgy once told our class, "If you can't or don't know how to host a dinner party, you have no right to preside at the Eucharist." Though the analogy can be taken too far, he was making the point that, in Christ's name, the presider should prepare the space, attend to all the details in advance, create a hospitable environment, welcome the assembly, enable them to hear the story and share their own, create a community from the congregating individuals, and send them out fed, refreshed, and encouraged.

Fulton Sheen was correct: "It's the Mass that matters"—then, now, and for eternity to come.

3

Confirmation

Mr. Brown's BBQ

I MAY BE THE only priest to tell you this, but in writing *The Da Vinci Code*, Dan Brown did Christianity a favor. Seventy percent of the book was well researched, while the rest of it was utter nonsense. Dan was not writing Christian history; he was writing a novel, so he could write anything he wanted. His timing was marketing genius. Here was a novel claiming to expose the Catholic Church's greatest secret twelve weeks after Cardinal Bernard Law of Boston was forced to resign on December 13, 2002, because of the cover-up of cases involving clergy sexual abuse. It wasn't hard for a cynical public to believe that the Catholic Church had been covering up sex scandals for all its history, beginning with Jesus and Mary Magdalene.

Mr. Brown wrote so authoritatively that a largely theologically uneducated public bought it entirely. During the time that the novel and film were at the height of their selling powers, I lost count of the number of barbecues I attended where, within minutes of receiving a burger and a beer, someone would ask me, "Father, have you read *The Da Vinci Code*?" and I would spend the next three hours talking about Jesus and Mary Magdalene, the formation of the New Testament, the baptism of Emperor Constantine, and the Dead Sea Scrolls. Name me another saint, pope, or theologian who has been able to get those topics discussed at contemporary cookouts? Dan did.

His greatest favor was to inform, through his novel, believer and unbeliever alike that, after having issued the Edict of Milan in February 313 that brought toleration of Christianity throughout the Roman Empire, the baptism of Emperor Constantine on his deathbed in 337 paved the way in 380 for Emperor Theodosius I to decree that the empire was now to be solely Christian.

All this has a direct bearing on the sacraments of initiation. Until the Edict of Milan, Christianity was often a persecuted sect, and therefore numbers were relatively small. The local bishop served as a modern-day pastor, the ordinary minister of most sacraments, especially regarding the sacraments of initiation. Until the early fourth century, baptism, Eucharist, and confirmation were administered together by the bishop. Following the edict of tolerance, the threat of martyrdom ceased, the ranks of Christians swelled dramatically, and small dioceses overseen by local bishops expanded rapidly. With this quick and sharp expansion, the bishops could not keep up with the increase in converts and became more concerned with governing a larger area and organizing more people. Consequently, the bishops of the western part of the empire delegated the administering of the sacraments of baptism and Eucharist to their priests. In the intervening centuries, especially as a smaller number of adults were baptized compared to children, bishops retained the administering of confirmation as a way of later "confirming" the initiation of the one who had earlier been baptized and admitted to the table of the Lord. It was a way of connecting the neophyte to the one, wider Christian family. Over the centuries, various customs persisted, especially regarding the age of confirmation. By the ninth century, the custom in the West that we retain mostly today became normative practice and was finally legislated at the Fourth Lateran Council in the thirteenth century.

The bishops in the eastern part of the empire came up with another solution. They chose not to divide up the sacraments of initiation, even though they, too, were dealing with waves of aspirants seeking to be baptized. They delegated their priests to celebrate all three sacraments in the one ritual. This continues to be the practice in the Orthodox churches. For Eucharist, the priest takes the consecrated bread, dips it into the consecrated wine, and spoons it into the mouth of the communicant. This enables babies to receive holy communion easily. Interestingly, after their baptisms, children do not usually receive the Eucharist again until, like their Western peers, they have received instructions about this sacrament and are seven or eight years of age.

Today in the West, baptism, Eucharist, and confirmation are three separate actions of the one journey into full communion with the community of faith in Jesus Christ, so that "it gives us a special strength of the Holy Spirit to spread and defend the faith by word and action as true witnesses of Christ, to confess the name of Christ boldly, and never to be ashamed of the Cross" (*CCC* §1303).

A Soldier for Christ

For some time, confirmation has been a sacrament looking for a purpose. Some dioceses follow the most ancient practice of placing it before the reception of the Eucharist, but this often involves receiving either confirmation at an early age or Eucharist later. Aware of the venerable and various ancient customs, the law regarding the timing of confirmation is left to the local bishop. For some, it also raises the question of when penance should be administered, either before a young person makes his or her holy communion and confirmation or afterward, but more on that in the next chapter.

Over generations, confirmation has acted like a quasi-puberty ritual, a Catholic bar mitzvah for boys and bat mitzvah for girls. As important as these ages are, and as necessary as rituals around puberty should be, historically it is a difficult for confirmation to perform this function. But this is often how it has been presented. At the age of thirteen, I was instructed that we were going to become "adults in the faith" and "soldiers for Christ." The bishop's involvement added gravitas to the occasion. We were so rehearsed about what to do and what not to do at the ceremony that I was terrified of making a mistake—and with worthy cause. The bishop who confirmed me was well known to correct a teenager publicly if he thought the person was not paying attention to his long and convoluted homily. He also did on-the-spot changes to saints' names that he didn't know or like (girls always got Mary and boys got Joseph), and he would bark instructions at the accompanying priests if the ceremony wasn't going to his satisfaction. It was a very stressful occasion for all concerned except the bishop.

In the preparation for the ceremony and in the bishop's homily, we were constantly told that the sacrament of confirmation would make us soldiers for Christ. This image has a long history. St. Cyril of Jerusalem is the first person recorded as using it in relation to confirmation in AD 350. His timing is significant. At the time, people knew, within living memory, of Christians who had been martyred for the faith. Although St. Paul addressed other Christians as fellow soldiers in his letters to the Philippians and Philemon, the earliest community did not need a reminder about the potential cost in fighting the good fight. As we have noted, by the fourth century, life for Christians was changing for the better, so Cyril was at pains to remind the new Christians that the fight goes on, and even though one may not be asked to give one's life, there was still a battle to be waged between good and evil, and a price to be paid for being under the standard of Christ. Wonderfully, there remains a ritual gesture at confirmation that comes from this period and is about toughening up for the ensuing fight. Until 1970, the bishop used to impose hands on the candidates' heads and then "gently strike" his or her face while saying, "Peace be with you." Although some sources state that a slap to the face was delivered in the ritual commissioning of foot soldiers in the Roman army in the fourth century, it appears that William Durandus inserted the ritual in the thirteenth century based on the analogy of the "buffet": the ceremonial blow ("dubbing" in England) that was conferred when knighting medieval squires. At confirmation, it was intended to be a pang of pain to remind the confirmati that they will pay a price for spreading Christ's peace. Maybe for good reasons, this ritual act has been adapted to a simple exchange of the more genial sign of peace.

I liked being a soldier for Christ. It made more sense than being told we were going to become "adults for Christ" (the bar mitzvah idea), because most of us knew we were still going to be treated as children at home and at school. Standing up and being counted for our faith, hope, and love was important as we entered puberty, and while it's good that we have moved from these militaristic metaphors, reminding all Christians of the cost of faith is still worthwhile since we always stand on the shoulders of the martyrs.

While the Eastern churches, in not separating confirmation from baptism and Eucharist, have preserved the better and more ancient tradition, it is not as though the creative and confirming action of the Holy Spirit is not present.

The word *Spirit* appears nearly four hundred times in the Old Testament. The Hebrew word is *ruah* and the Greek is *pneuma* ("to blow, to breathe," from which we get the word *pneumonia*, where we struggle to breathe), and the Spirit is often portrayed as a powerful wind, the breath of life, or divine inspiration. From the first chapter of Genesis, God's Spirit hovers over the water (Gen 1:2). Throughout the Old Testament, this same Spirit filled Moses with the skill, perception, and knowledge of every kind of craft (Exod 31:3–4); brought true justice to the nations (Isa 42:1); and, as a foretaste of the resurrection, breathed new life into the dead in the Valley of Dry Bones (Ezek 37:1–14).

In recent years, biblical scholars have rediscovered the importance of how the Spirit in the Old Testament is often called Wisdom, a feminine verb. Wisdom is the personification of God's action in the world. "For wisdom is more mobile than any motion; because of her pureness she pervades and penetrates all things....Although she is but one, she can do all things, and while remaining in herself, she renews all things; in every generation she passes into holy souls and makes them friends of God, and prophets....She is more beautiful than the sun.... Compared with the light she is found to be superior, for it is succeeded by the night, but against wisdom evil does not prevail. She reaches mightily from one end of the earth to the other, and she orders all things well" (Wis 7:24—8:1). To encounter Wisdom was to encounter God. Later, the Greek word *Sophia* was translated as "Wisdom."

One of the least recognized but very important developments in the action of the Spirit comes in the New Testament, especially in John's Gospel, where the Hebrew tradition of the Spirit is expressed as the Logos or Word of God that takes human form in Jesus. Gerald O'Collins and Mario Farrugia have explained:

> The Logos or Word of God converged with Wisdom as another OT divine personification that foreshadowed the distinct existence of a second person in God. Like Lady Wisdom, the Word was understood to be with God and powerfully creative from the beginning (Gen 1:1—2:4; Isa 55:10–11). The psalms, in particular, celebrated the creative and conserving Word of God (e.g. Ps 33:8–9). Sirach appreciated how the divine Word operates to conserve creation: by God's Word "all things hold together" (Sir 43:26)....Naming God as "Father," "Son" (Word and Wisdom), and "Spirit" found its roots in the Old Testament. There "wisdom," "word," and "spirit" functioned, frequently synonymously, to acknowledge God's nearness to the world and to the chosen people.[1]

Participating in Pentecost

Confirmation clearly inherits its identity from Pentecost. There are two Pentecost traditions in the Gospels. The first one is the same day as the resurrection. John writes, "When he had said this, he breathed on them and said to them, 'Receive the Holy Spirit'" (John 20:22). Breathing upon the disciples is a quotation of Genesis 2:7, when God "breathed into [the] nostrils" of the first human beings the "breath of life." Here, in breaking the power of death, Christ re-creates humanity and sends them out to live this life in the world. It is significant that the first manifestation of this life that Christ mentions is forgiveness: "If you forgive the sins of any, they are forgiven them; if you retain the sins of any, they are retained" (John 20:23). More on this in the next chapter.

The story of the first Pentecost in Acts 2 has had the most impact on our understanding of confirmation. Some people erroneously believe we "receive the Holy Spirit" at confirmation. The Spirit, which is with us from our conception and birth, is named, called forth, and celebrated in baptism. In this sacrament, we confirm our life in the Spirit and the mission to which we are sent. Patrick Fahey writes, "The Second Vatican Council taught that in confirmation, we 'are endowed with the special strength of the Holy Spirit,' 'are bound more intimately to the Church,' and 'are more strictly obliged to spread the faith by word and deed' (*Lumen Gentium* 11)."[2]

Here, the story in the story is very instructive. The word *Pentecost* comes from the Greek word *pentēkostē*, meaning "fiftieth," and refers to the fiftieth day after Easter Sunday at the end of the seventh week. Numbers matter in the Bible. In the Old Testament, fifty was the year of jubilee because it was rare for people to live beyond their fiftieth birthday. That's why three score and ten (seventy) is such a huge age in the Bible. Very few people ever got there. Once in every lifetime, Israel marked a year of celebration. This is where and why we have twenty-five-, fifty-, and one-hundred-year jubilees to this day.

Of the many features of the Jubilee Year in Israel, three were consistent: they set slaves free; they cancelled the debts; and they let the fields for crops lie fallow. This meant that there was no such thing as a lifetime of slavery among the Israelites; there was no structural cross-generational poverty; and they cared for the environment. Is it any wonder that the power of the Spirit is unleashed on the fiftieth day? We have been set free from the slavery of our sin by Christ, all our debts have been forgiven in Christ, and we are recreated as a new creation through Christ. Applying this to the sacrament of confirmation means that as we experience our own personal Pentecost, we are meant to live as free sons and daughters of God, who forgive as we have been for-given, and to care for God's creation.

The second element of the story in the Acts of the Apostles is equally challenging for confirmation. If you're like me, you have been taught that the most public gift on display at the first Pentecost was that the apostles had the ability to speak in different tongues. A more careful reading of the story, however, reveals that the gift received that day was one equally of hearing as much as it may have been of speaking. Luke recounts, "In our own languages we hear them speaking about God's deeds of power" (Acts 2:11). It wasn't so much the gift of tongues the earliest disciples received as much as their hearers received the gift of "ears," of listening.

When it comes to listening in the church today, some people mistake mono for stereo, uniformity for unity. At the first Pentecost, the earliest Christians had no such difficulty; they knew that speaking the same language was not as important as carefully listening to one another. The early church community was very complex and diverse. Like today, they had great struggles both within and outside the com-munity. Within a few years of the first Pentecost, there were fights between Peter and Paul over Jewish and Gentile converts. There were people who died for the faith and others who betrayed them to the authorities. Some Christians thought they were for Paul or Apollos rather than for Jesus, and others thought the end of the world was nigh. The earliest Christian community was not a utopia.

Pentecost faith celebrated in an explicit way at the sacrament of confirmation holds that while we build our faith on the believers who have gone before us, we have the responsibility to listen to our con-temporary culture and put it into conversation with the gospel. That's why courage is one of the Holy Spirit's preeminent gifts. We are not to retreat from the world, but are sent out to dialogue with it, affirm-ing what we can and unashamedly standing against whatever demeans, oppresses, and is life denying. Therefore we need to ask the Holy Spirit to hone our ears as well as prepare our tongues to clearly receive and proclaim the gospel of Christ in the market places of our own time. To speak of the things of God to an increasingly secular world requires prudence and wisdom, listening before speaking.

As Acts 2 continues, more traces of the Holy Spirit are evident. In fact, by the end of the account of the first Pentecost, we are given a list of the signs of the followers of Jesus: wonders were being worked through them; they shared their goods with one another and with the poor; they praised God in the temple; they broke the bread at home; and they welcomed into their community those who received their message of salvation.

Confirmation can be reclaimed as the moment where the Holy Spirit, having embraced us at baptism, enables us to do the following: take Christ's Spirit as our own; listen before we speak; be open to wonder; share, especially with the poor; be filled with praise for how God works in and through the world; discover Christ's unique presence in the "breaking of the bread"; and show joyful hospitality. If we all lived out this call with courage, prudence, and wisdom, then the sacrament of confirmation would indeed re-create us and renew the face of the earth.

The Signs of the Spirit

If the first Pentecost was about hearing and speaking, it quickly became about being filled with wonder, sharing, praising God, breaking the bread, and receiving others with joy. If we really believe the Holy Spirit is confirmed in us through this sacrament, then this impressive series of outcomes should be present among us here and now.

First, a story. I admire our charismatic friends very much. They rightly love the Holy Spirit. I especially admire our Evangelical brothers and sisters not only because they have great faith, but also because they have great courage. When I see them in any public space actively witnessing to the faith, I know I could not do what they do.

Mind you, I am not sure what it is about me. I must have the word *pagan* emblazoned across my forehead, for every time I enter a shopping center and am minding my own business, I am accosted by our

Evangelical friends. Almost invariably they come up to me and ask, "Brother, have you given your life to Jesus Christ as your personal Lord and Savior?"

"Well, as a matter of fact I have."

"Has the Holy Spirit given you the gift of tongues?"

"Yes, but I choose not to use it because I don't find it a helpful means of communication."

"Do you know the demands of living the life of the Lord?"

"Well, I hope poverty, chastity, and obedience for Christ for life is a decent push in the right direction."

Mind you, in mentioning poverty, I am reminded of my family, who, on seeing Jesuit real estate for the first time when I took my vows of poverty, chastity, and obedience, said, "If this is poverty, I'd like to see how you guys live chastity—it all looks fast and loose to us."

In his Letter to the Galatians, St. Paul says that the action of the Holy Spirit comes in the way we are loving, joyful, peaceful, patient, kind, generous, faithful, gentle, and self-controlled. The problem with lists is that they can be nice in themselves but too removed from feeling a need to act upon them. The first Pentecost and the subsequent activity of the Holy Spirit, however, tells us that the hallmarks of the presence of God is not in our words but in how we stand in the public square. While it can be daunting, St. Paul makes it practical—that it is all about what we choose because that is what we become.

If we were charged for the crime of following the Holy Spirit in our daily choices, would there be enough evidence to convict us?

Pope St. John XXIII hoped there would be "a new Pentecost" at Vatican II where we recovered the most ancient tradition in our faith, and we see in various, unexpected, and inculturated ways the Holy Spirit has been present in all peoples, in every culture, that whenever the gospel has been proclaimed in a new land, it already compliments the best in that culture when it seeks to affirm personal dignity, human worth, justice, care of the earth, and the promotion of forgiveness and peace.

An issue that I have with Christian Evangelicals is that they often think the Holy Spirit can be primarily reduced to external signs. We know, however, from the first Pentecost and from our own confirmation that the Spirit works in both unpredictable and ordinary ways. The Holy Spirit, sent to live with us, continues to reveal God's truth to us, to advocate for us, and, in turn, to glorify us in Christ. The Spirit seems to make a specialty of being present in the unexpected.

Recalling that caring for the creation was one of the signs of the Year of Jubilee, it is an especially contemporary challenge if confirmation becomes the moment where we reflect upon and act on our moral obligations to care for creation, to treat it as the gift it is. In *Laudato Sí*, Pope Francis reminds us that we are called to be stewards, not wreckers of God's good gifts:

> If the simple fact of being human moves people to care for the environment of which they are a part, Christians in their turn realize that their responsibility within creation, and their duty towards nature and the Creator, are an essential part of their faith. (no. 64)

> Our insistence that each human being is an image of God should not make us overlook the fact that each creature has its own purpose. None is superfluous. The entire material universe speaks of God's love, his boundless affection for us. Soil, water, mountains: everything is, as it were, a caress of God. (no. 84)

> A healthy relationship with creation is one dimension of overall personal conversion, which entails the recognition of our errors, sins, faults and failures, and leads to heartfelt repentance and desire to change. (no. 218)

> The universe unfolds in God, who fills it completely. Hence, there is a mystical meaning to be found in a leaf, in a mountain trail, in a dewdrop, in a poor person's face. The ideal is not only to pass from the exterior to the interior to discover

the action of God in the soul, but also to discover God in all things. (no. 233)

Rather than see Pope Francis's words in any idiosyncratic or exotic way, our care for the earth is one of the first fruits of the Holy Spirit being confirmed in us, an ancient traditional and biblical responsibility.

Finding God's Traces

Continuous with our right and harmonious relationship with the earth is the right ordering of our own lives. If a contemporary approach to the sacrament of confirmation holds anything, it is in the church's venerable tradition of the gift of discernment, to finding the action of the Holy Spirit in the impact of our personal decisions in our daily lives.

St. Ignatius Loyola understood this sacrament well. He left the church a guide for working out how we can tell if and where the Holy Spirit is leading us. From my reading on what he says about discernment in his *Spiritual Exercises*, his letters, and other writings, here are my twelve contemporary spins on his timeless wisdom about how to minimize evil in our lives and avoid sin and destructive behavior by making good choices.

1. *Trust the commonplace, the ordinary, the every day.* Live in the here and now. Sometimes we live in an unhealed past or an unknown future, whereas God may be found right under our nose, in the here and now. The good spirit draws us to deal with our ordinary life, as it is, not as we may like it to be, and to discern his presence there. We often look for God in the spectacular and extraordinary, whereas he is often to be found in the quiet and mundane moments and comes to us poor, naked, in prison, hungry, and thirsty. We need to be wary of false consolation. "The good can be the enemy of the better." We are attacked at the most vulnerable parts of

ourselves and allured by the narcotics of modern living (drugs, alcohol, sex, work, gambling, technology, and shopping), which never take away the pain of living but temporarily mask its effects.

2. *Do not make a decision when feeling down; allow the crisis to pass.* Sometimes we make the worst decisions when we are under pressure. It is always better to let a crisis pass, and then, in calmer surroundings, weigh up all the options.

3. *Be suspicious of "the urgent."* Sometimes we need to make a big decision quickly. Buying some time, any time, is always helpful for working out the best course of action. The good spirit brings a sense of perspective and priority to problems. We need to be especially careful of making a life-changing decision that goes against another life choice made properly in a time of consolation or peace.

4. *Be humble enough to take wise advice.* We are not meant to be "rocks and islands," operating on our own. We need the wisdom of our families and most trusted friends, the church, and sometimes professionals to inform our consciences and make the best possible decisions before God. Remember that the word *obedience* comes from the Latin word *obedire*, meaning "to listen." If we all want to be obedient to God's reign in our world and lives, we need to get good at listening, in all its forms, because we believe that God listens to and hears us.

5. *There are always patterns to the action of the good and evil spirits in our lives.* Sometimes we think something "came out of nowhere." Sometimes it does, but most times, the good and bad that beset us have a history and a context. We need to train ourselves to read the signs of both, cultivate the things that are good, and see the empty promises of the bad spirit and how it can lead us into dead ends. A daily examination of conscience helps us to see the pattern of the Holy Spirit.

6. *The signs of the good spirit* are courage, strength, consolation, inspiration, and peace, feeling as though obstacles can be overcome and that we are worth something and can contribute good things to the world. St. Paul also has a very helpful list in Galatians: "The fruit of the Spirit is love, joy, peace, patience, kindness, generosity, faithfulness, gentleness, and self-control" (Gal 5:22–23). The signs of the bad spirit are sadness, obstacles that seem insurmountable, lack of self-worth, turmoil, impulsiveness, negativity, agitations, and regularly giving into temptations.

7. *A good or better decision is just one decision away.* The bad spirit always convinces us that we are trapped and there is no way out, diminishing our memory so we keep repeating destructive behavior even though it never helps. It alienates us and does not help us deal with our situation. A journal can help wherein we review our life and its patterns with compassion and courage. For major decisions requiring discernment, we can draw up a list on one side of the page with the movements for A and the movements for B, with the movements against A and the movements against B on the other side. The process does not focus on which list is the longest, but where our heart and head is drawn.

8. *The good spirit connects us and frees us up to be more open.* The evil spirit divides, isolates, and locks us in our fears. Every time we are transparent with those we love and trust, the good spirit is at work. There is nothing we have ever done, are doing, or will do, that will stop God from loving us. There is nothing that God cannot forgive and heal, but we need to be honest about who we are and what we have done. Then, anything and everything is possible.

9. *The Holy Spirit is always present where a community of faith in God gathers.* In the community, we discover that

we are not the only ones who have ever had to make a choice or to face similar problems.

10. *Get our heads and hearts in dialogue—we need both.* Some believers think that Christian faith is cerebral. While theology has a venerable intellectual tradition and thinking clearly is very important, our heads need to be in touch with our affective lives and instincts. When our head and heart are more integrated, we have a good chance at putting our hands and feet in a place where we will do the greatest good for the greatest number. Our head can be filled with dreams, some of them good. Our heart and gut can hold desires. Which persist? Which ones lose their appeal over time? What are our deepest desires?

11. *No work for the coming of the kingdom is too small, irrelevant, or inconsequential.* We can often be conned into thinking that our relatively small and daily acts of kindness do not count for much in the overall spiritual scheme. Wrong! If there were more evil actions than loving actions in our world on any one day, the earth would be personally unlivable. Simple and selfless acts of kindness might go unreported, but they change the world by enabling Christ's love to break through into the world of our daily lives.

12. *Fidelity is one of the greatest gifts of the Spirit.* Even in the face of opposition and other choices, remaining faithful is a heroic act of love. That said, the gospel calls us to "die unto self," not to "kill self." It is never God's will, for example, for a person to stay in a physically, emotionally, and spiritually violent relationship. Ignatius encourages us to imagine we are advising our best friend about the matter we have under discernment. What would your counsel be? Alternatively, imagine being on your deathbed. In reviewing your life, what choices do you

wish you had made? Hopefully, every choice would be
the most loving, faithful, and hopeful one.

Confirmation is about experiencing the power and love of the
Spirit as an intensely practical affair in the choices we make every day,
and how those choices create who we are in Christ.

Note that in John's Gospel, when Christ appears after being raised
from the dead, not only does he breathe the Holy Spirit upon the disciples, he also gives them the gift of peace. In fact, peace is his primary
Easter gift.

No wonder peace is one of the Spirit's preeminent gifts. Have you
noticed how many people answer the question "How are you?" by saying,
"I'm tired, exhausted, finished, or spent." And that's the day they return
from vacation! Alternatively, they say, "I'm frantic, run off my feet, there
are not enough hours in the day." We all seem to be frantic or exhausted.
How do we know this is right? When was the last time you asked a friend
how they were and they replied, "I've got the life/work balance perfectly
in order—thanks for asking"? We never hear that. I wonder what would
happen if we replied, "Relaxed and laid back" or "Taking time to smell the
roses." I don't think we would be believed, or we might get a lecture from
our friends on how lucky we are not to be busy!

Sometimes there's a competition about who can be the most
exhausted and the most frantic. One of my friends always has to be the
busiest person he knows. If I ever say I have been busy lately, he will
reply, "You're busy? I'm run off my feet!" And I want to say, "John, I'm
sorry, I should've realized we're playing the 'I'm the busiest person in
the room competition' and I know you always have to win that one."

As Christians we must be careful about this busyness competition.
Being active in our lives and engaged with the world around us is a gift,
but if we are honest about our busyness, some of it is not virtuous. It's
about denial, avoidance, or trying to compete with our peer group. It's
curious that just as we all compete to be the busiest person we know, we
also complain that what we really want is "some peace and quiet." We
can't have it both ways. Compulsive, frantic activity is the enemy of peace.

Sometimes we can think that peace and quiet is sitting in the lotus position in a darkened room. It can be, but Christ's gift of peace is more robust. Peace is like all the best things in life: an attitude of mind and a habit born of consistently making good choices. Some people can do a large amount of work and be quite serene. Peace, for them, is a way of life—of being a contemplative in action.

Seneca, a first-century philosopher, noticed how most of his friends and acquaintances were lacking peace. He wrote a famous book on anger and how to deal with it. He especially noticed that his richest friends were the angriest of all. Seneca came to believe that the reason so many people were agitated was that they had an unreasonable expectation about how smoothly their day would go. Those who were rich thought their money would buy them an easier life in every way, and when it didn't, they got the angriest of all. If Seneca is right and we want more peace and quiet, we must have realistic expectations of each day and factor in the things that might go wrong.

If our confirmation leads us to live more contemplative lives, it would be entirely in continuity with the first manifestation of the Holy Spirit when the apostles were confirmed for their mission.

Gifts of the Spirit

Because the Spirit's gifts are given fully at baptism, theologians have had to consider how any other gifts can be added at confirmation. Eventually they argued that, using the same oil of chrism as is used at baptism, the gifts of the Spirit are "sealed" in this third and final moment of initiation. In the ancient world, oil was used to strengthen and heal. The word *chrism* comes from the Greek word *chrisma*, meaning "to anoint," and is also the same root word for *Christ*. It is the church's holiest oil, the only one to which fragrance is added, and is used at the Christian coronation of kings and queens, the ordination of priests and bishops, and the sacraments of baptism and confirmation. These uses underline how these rituals set the candidate apart for a special Christian mission. Anointing a candidate at confirmation strengthens the effect of baptism and reminds them that they are anointed to a special call to live what they profess.

Mirroring the seven petitions in the Lord's Prayer, the seven Beatitudes, and the seven last words of Jesus from the cross, the seven gifts of the Holy Spirit are wisdom, understanding, counsel, fortitude, knowledge, piety, and fear of the Lord.

Tony Kelly offers a contemporary approach to each of them: Wisdom gives us a deep experience of the mystery of God: the opportunity to "taste and see that the LORD is good" (Ps 34:8). Understanding gives us an intuitive grasp of the essence of the faith; and the ability to communicate the meaning of the Gospel in clear, brief, and telling terms. Right judgment (counsel) gives us the right "feel" for a given situation so that we are guided through it with a peaceful, intuitive assurance to decide rightly as, for example, in matters of justice and the domain of human relations. Courage (fortitude) is that which the Holy Spirit breathes into our hearts, giving us the strength to think big and to put our best and most imaginative selves into the task before us. It is most obvious in the witness of martyrs who have died for their faith. Knowledge is a special capacity to see through pretensions and keep a sense of proportion; it lets us see the world as it really is. Awe and wonder give us the power to remember and appreciate the greatness of God: to breathe deeply and live lightly in an atmosphere of gracious mystery. Fear of the Lord is about the reverence we have in our personal relationship with Christ giving us the power to love God, each other, and indeed all creation.[3]

Added to these seven "special" gifts, St. Paul says that the Holy Spirit's gifts are encouragement, different tongues, healing, interpretation of tongues, the power to distinguish spirits, practical service, leadership, prophecy, teaching, the working of miracles, intense faith, knowledge, and wisdom (see Rom 12:6–8; 1 Cor 12:8–10). And, as if that isn't enough, St. Paul, in writing to the community of Galatia, the area around modern-day Ankara, Turkey (ca. AD 50), says that if the Holy Spirit is manifest in our lives, we will be marked by being loving, joyful, peaceful, patient, kind, generous, faithful, gentle, and self-controlled (see Gal 5:22–23).

The gifts outlined above are as exhaustive as they would be exhausting if we lived them all the time, as good as that would be. However, we are sinful and frail and often do not live up to the best of that which is given to us by God. These gifts are also goals and challenges for us. Therefore, in a comparable way to baptism, we are invited to take a patron saint to pray with us and for us, and to urge us on and to inspire us to live the Christian life in the same way that they fought the good fight. It might be that we take our baptismal saint, but more often, it's an opportunity for us to marry the great tradition of the cloud of witnesses to our own experience and invite a patron saint to enable us to finish the race confirmed in the Spirit.

Of Gods and Men

Given that confirmation emerges from the era of the martyrs, the 2011 film *Of Gods and Men* is a contemporary cinematic parable portraying the action of the Holy Spirit. Certainly this film may be one of the finest religious films ever made. Based on the 2002 book *The Monks of Tibhirine* by John Kiser,[4] the film was written and directed by Xavier Beauvois.

John Kiser's book told the wider story, but the 2010 film about the community and its end, was where, along with the rest of the world, I came to know, only in part, and to admire in full the nine heroic men of that religious community. Two survived. One was Fr. Jean Pierre, who is quoted as saying, "I was in my room, in the porter's lodge, out a bit from the seclusion area. I heard some noises. I thought that the terrorists came to look for medicines as they had done before. I did not move until someone came to knock at my door. I was frightened. But I opened it. It was a priest from the Orano diocese who came to tell me that my fellow brothers had been kidnapped. It was a shock, as hard as my sense of confusion. But at the beginning no one thought that they could harm some monks, men of prayer respected by everyone." Fr. Amédée also survived. Through both men we know in detail what happened before and during the night of March 27, 1996.

In 2010, the film won the Jury Prize at the Cannes Film Festival and later won awards from the International Cinephile Society, London Critics Circle Film, the U.S. National Board of Review, and the César Awards of 2011. Slow and deliberate, this film initiates us both into the world of the Catholic Trappist Monastery of Mt. Atlas, as well as into the life of postcolonial Algeria with its corrupt government, extreme Islamist terrorists imposing something like Taliban terror on the local towns and villages, and the ambiguous role of the military.

The Order of Cistercians of the Strict Observance is a monastic community that follows the Rule of St. Benedict. Founded in 1664, they are a reform movement of the Benedictine tradition, living the Rule, as their name suggests, much more strictly. The Benedictine Rule breaks up the day into periods for liturgy, community life, meals, reading, and work, where the regular rhythm of life enables the monk or nun to come closer to God. The rigor of Benedictine monasteries is not easy, but Benedict's rule is marked by its gentle tone and compassion "to establish a school for the Lord's service"[5] where "we progress in this way of life [that, in his love, God shows us] and in faith," and so "run along the way of God's commandments, our hearts overflowing with the inexpressible delight of love" so that "never swerving from his instructions, but faithfully observing his teaching in the monastery until death, we shall through patience share in the passion of Christ that we may deserve also to share in his Kingdom."[6]

St. Benedict understood the link between liturgy and life. He thought that living life at a less breakneck speed was sane, and he was passionate about savoring things—actions, food, creation, people, and especially words.

Of Gods and Men communicates the life and spirit of that community: the prayer, Eucharist, sung liturgy, silence and contemplation, the detachment enhanced by the vow of poverty, the taken-for-granted sacrifices of the vow of chastity, the work, the meals, the readings, the meetings, and social outreach.

What was distinctive about the Trappist monastery at Tibhirine was their interaction with and service of the local Islamic community. The monks were generally loved and respected by their neighbors. They sold their honey and vegetables in the local market, worked to help build houses, and gave any support they could to those in need. Brother Luc, however, was a medical doctor who ran a clinic and dispensary from the monastery. He was the only trained doctor in the area. He served the villages, wounded rebels and soldiers alike.

It is Brother Luc's letters back to France that gives us the most vivid picture of the impending threats. Despite the local esteem with which they were held, the monks were Catholic and French. The rebels sometimes attacked their monastery and regularly made threats. They were frightened, and the religious men seriously contemplated leaving the country. Brother Luc wrote, "The violence here has not abated. How can we get out of this mess? Violence will not cure violence. We can only exist as humans by becoming symbols of love, as manifested in Christ, who, though himself just, submitted himself to injustice."[7]

We now know that the monks had to discern personally and corporately whether to stay or go. In the film, and according to the eyewitness accounts, they had vigorous community meetings at which they weighed the options. They looked at what impact their decision would have on their families, the local people, and the opportunity to continue their work elsewhere. One of the monks is traumatized by the enormity of the choice to stay or go and endures a "dark night of the soul." His conversation with the prior is one of the most moving scenes in an already moving film. In the end, each monk decides to stay, not because anyone wants an untimely or gruesome death, but because their solidarity with the local community, their work for justice, and their witness to Christ's resurrection and life means that to cut and run would be a betrayal.

Through the accounts of Frs. Jean Pierre and Amédée, we know that the night before their confreres were abducted, the eight monks at

Tibhirine were joined by a ninth monk, Fr. Bruno, from the community at Morocco near Fez. He arrived to oversee the election of the prior. He brought with him gifts of wine and cheese. It occasioned a celebratory meal, which was to be their last supper. We know they listened to one of the only tape recordings they had, Tchaikovsky's *Swan Lake*. The actual music we hear in the film is from the scene in the ballet where Odette, the white swan, realizes she will always be entrapped because Prince Siegfried has been deceived by the evil scheming of Odile, the black swan. Odette dies and, shortly after, so does Siegfried, so that in death they achieve the consummation that life could only frustrate. As the wordless scene of the monk's last supper continues in the film, the faces of the men tell the story of the life and death choice that they will soon consummate.

After 1:00 a.m. on March 27, Fr. Christian, Brother Luc, Fr. Christophe, Brother Michel, Fr. Bruno, Fr. Célestin, and Brother Paul were abducted at gun point. Fr. Jean Pierre was never discovered living in the porter's lodge. As the terrorists searched the monastery, Fr. Amédée hid under his bed, which resulted in his escape. He died in 2008.

Fr. Christian's last journal entry is from the night he was abducted:

> My death, obviously, will appear to justify those who hastily judged me naive or idealistic....But these must know that at last my most insistent curiosity will be satisfied. For this is what I shall be able to do, if God wills: immerse my gaze in that of the Father to contemplate with him his children of Islam as he sees them....And you, too, my last-minute friend, who would not have known what you were doing; yes, for you too I say this thank-you and this—to commend you to the God in whose face I see in yours. And may he grant to us to find each other in Paradise, if it please God, the Father of us both. Amen! Inshallah!

Though the monks could have escaped to safer Morocco and then onto France, their discernment of the Holy Spirit's leadings was to stay faithful to their peaceful and loving life as a counterwitness to the hatred and terror that surrounded them. Sustained and formed by a lifetime of daily prayer, Eucharist, and constantly striving to live the Holy Spirit's seven gifts and fruits, they knew they had to remain constant to their faith, hope, and love in Jesus, and witness as he did to justice and peace as that may claim everything from them. Like Christ, the monks did not seek to die; they were killed because of their witness, faith, and trust in the Holy Spirit.

One of the most surprisingly moving moments in this film occurs at the end when Fr. Bruno, the visitor, *angelorum* in Latin, having borne gifts for body, mind, and spirit is frog-marched out to death along with his other six brothers. He had not been part of the process of spiritual discernment with the others. He was in the wrong place at the worst time. As Fr. Bruno was taken away, Fr. Amédée, from under his bed, heard Bruno say to his captors, "But I am just a visitor." Fr. Bruno is the patron saint of all of us—visitors on this earth until we make the final journey home. On January 26, 2018, Pope Francis signed the decree paving the way for these men to be beatified, the immediate step before being canonized a saint. The ceremony was held at Oran, Algeria, on December 8, 2018.

For Christians, the sacrament of confirmation is the ritual sealing of the Holy Spirit given at baptism that initiates us into a lifetime of discerning the Spirit's call and enabling us to face the consequences with faith, hope, and love.

4

Penance

FOR A SACRAMENT that is all about healing, reconciliation, and forgiveness, there are few Catholic rituals that elicit such a strong and often negative response. Admittedly, my own first experience of it was not the best.

My grade one and two teacher, Sister Mary Consuelo, prepared me for my first confession. She was five feet tall and four feet wide. Behind her back, we called her Sister Mary-consume-a-whale-o. She was firm and fair. She needed to be. She once told me that in the forty-four years of her teaching career, she never had less than forty children in her class. In 1959, she had sixty-one children in the same room. There were forty-two children in my first grade class in 1969. Can you imagine that ratio now? In the first grade, sister prepared us for our first confession and our first holy communion. I remember being so terrified going into the dark box to make my first confession, that when the slide pulled back, I could barely see through the grill. In my anxiety, I started yelling, "Bless me father for I have sinned, this is my first confession, and these are my sins." At that point, the dean of the cathedral said, "God's not deaf and neither am I!"

I wish I could say that I was really looking forward to my first holy communion because I wanted to receive the Lord in a special and unique way. But that would be a lie. Actually, I was terrified of doing something wrong during the Mass and of biting the host. At the age of seven, I was really looking forward to the party that followed the Mass and the presents I would receive. Back at school on the day after my communion, Sister Mary Consuelo asked me what gift I enjoyed the most. Of all the Bibles, holy pictures, rosaries, and medals I received, the gift I treasured most was a bone china holy water font of the Madonna and Child. "I would like to see that," Sister Mary Consuelo said. "Would you bring it to school tomorrow?"

The next day during the first break—"little lunch" we used to call it—sister was on playground duty. She was wearing a large blue and white striped apron over her habit. Imagine this scene. There were over seven hundred children in my Catholic primary school, and there was only one teacher supervising all of us—a ratio of 1:700. That would be illegal today. Not that Sister Mary-consume-a-whale-o had any trouble controlling the masses. She was a formidable figure who was as wide as she was tall and ruled the playground with a whistle. Do you remember how big the nun's pockets were in those habits? It seemed that nuns carried everything in them, and they could put their hands on what they needed at a moment's notice. I raced up to sister, who was surrounded by children. "I've brought the holy water font, sister." "Very good, go and get it." All wrapped up in tissue paper, I carefully took the font out of my bag and then ran down to the asphalt playground. I was so excited at showing off my favorite present that, right in front of sister, I tripped and down I went. The font hit the asphalt too. It did not break. No, it smashed into tiny pieces. Sister swung into action. She was an old hand at health and safety long before the term was invented. Into her pocket she went. Out came the whistle and with a full, shrill blast, seven hundred children froze in their spots. Sister said to the children in our vicinity, "Whoever picks up the most pieces of china will get a holy picture." We thought that was something back then.

The second whistle rang out, and while 650 children resumed their games, 50 children did a forensic search of the area, picking up every piece the naked eye could see and dropped them in the hammock that sister had made from her apron with her left arm. Meanwhile, in my distress, Consuelo's right arm brought me in for a very big hug. Sister had many gifts, but among them was a very ample bosom. In fact, whenever we read about God's deep and consoling breasts in Isaiah 66:11, I go back to grade one. With one action, I was enveloped in her very ample bosom. I couldn't breathe, and I wasn't sure I was ever going to get out of there alive. In fact, I think I made my decision to become a celibate priest at that moment.

When the bell rang, I was released from her profound embrace, and sister rolled up the apron and walked me back to class. Three weeks later, she told me to stay in at little lunch. I thought I was in trouble. When every other child had left the room, she opened the drawer of her desk and there, wrapped in new tissue paper, was a fully restored holy water font. By then I think I had forgotten about it.

In those days, we knew very little about the sisters: they went to Mass, said their prayers, and taught school. Before Sister Mary Consuelo became a nun, however, Helen Leane had done a degree in fine art, majoring in watercolors and ceramics. She had taken those hundreds of fragments and spent hours and hours piecing back together my holy water font. When it was set, she repainted the entire object. The only sign that it had ever been broken was the rough plaster of paris on the back. She could have thrown those pieces away and I would have gotten over it. In fact, I had. However, such was the effect of her prayer life on her relationships, even with a seven-year-old boy; she spent what must have been most of her leisure time for weeks reconstructing a treasured gift. But she was the real gift that day, and it was the best lesson I had from her.

While not an overly sentimental person when it comes to things, and having been privileged to have studied or worked in Australia, the United Kingdom, Italy, and the United States, nevertheless, everywhere I go to live, that font comes with me. Soon after being ordained a priest in December 1993, I was honored to be asked to preside at the Eucharist at Emmaus, the Sisters of Mercy nursing home in Brisbane. Sitting in her usual spot in the front row was Sister Mary Consuelo, now age ninety. As part of my homily, I told the other hundred sisters the story of the holy water font. When I was done and sat down, sister got up from her place and turned around to the others and said, "I told you I was good!" She was very good, indeed.

I visited her when I could over the next few years. My last visit with her was in early March 1996. At that time she knew she was dying. She talked about it openly and calmly. I asked her if she was frightened to die. "Oh no," she quickly retorted, "I'm frightened of pain, but I am not fearful of death because I have been praying all my life preparing for that final journey home when I hope to meet Christ face-to-face and hopefully hear him say, 'Well done, good and faithful servant—with what you had you did your best.'" As I drove away from her that final day, there was Helen in my rear vision mirror, now a frail wizened figure waving good-bye. I had tears streaming down my face in gratitude for a teacher who never stopped teaching, an adult who simply and appropriately loved kids who were not her own, and a believer who showed me that prayer is about living this life as fully as we can so that, when we come to die, it's an opportunity to hear Christ say, "With what you had you did your best." If that sort of confident faith is what a lifetime of attending the sacrament of penance and Eucharist gives you, then bring it on!

This story is instructive on several levels. Incidentally, the sacrament is called penance, not confession or the more positive name, reconciliation. The word *penance* discloses its long and complex history.

Rooted in the many times Jesus forgives sins and preaches long and hard that if we follow him we must forgive each other, including our enemies, the early church developed two related traditions. The first was a period of penance for people preparing to be initiated into the life of the church to be absolved of the sins of their past lives, so that they, and the community, could see them admitted to the table of the Lord free of any burdens that may have held them back from full membership.

The second tradition was a solution to a problem. In the age of the martyrs, there were Christians who betrayed others to the authorities. Their sin cost lives. After any period or time of persecution, the early church had to decide how to handle its betrayers and apostates. We know that some communities excluded their great sinners, especially if they did not heed any of the bishop's warnings. Other communities, mindful of Jesus's words and witness, developed a process by which they could reconcile their worst sinners into the life of the Christian community, and after a period of preparation, they would be readmitted to the Lord's table. It must have been no small thing to share Eucharist again with people who may have aided and abetted the death of your family and friends. Later, murder and adultery joined apostasy as public sins from which Christians could seek forgiveness from God and the community.

This penitential process was not easy or quick. To join the order of penitents, as it came to be called, a woman or man first had to confess privately to the bishop. Then they wore sackcloth as a public sign of their sorrow. During this period, they would sometimes perform very severe penances. For example, they were dismissed from the Mass after the Liturgy of the Word and would go and pray for the forgiveness of their sins. Then, usually on Holy Thursday night, the bishop would welcome them back to the Eucharist by imposing hands upon their heads and announcing to the assembly that they had been forgiven by Christ and reconciled to the community. This process was not for the fainthearted, and most importantly, it was only available once after baptism. It seems God may have been willing to forgive serious sinners, but he was not going to do it continually.

This last point had an impact on a person who will feature significantly in this book. In AD 313, Emperor Constantine became a catechumen, one preparing to enter into full communion with the church. However, he was not baptized until 337. The emperor put it off for years because he knew that, once baptized, he had a once-in-a-lifetime shot at being reconciled to the community. He was especially anxious that, as a commander of an army, he had committed the sin of murder, so, despite what *The Da Vinci Code* says, when he thought his death was imminent, and that he could probably sin no more, he asked for baptism, received holy communion, and later confessed his sins. As we have noted, this was a watershed moment for the church.

From the seventh century onward, monasteries flourished all over the Christian world and local people came seeking advice and spiritual direction. This often involved the telling of their sins not with the long and complex process of the order of penitents, but by making a private confession. This also led to priests absolving sins privately. This development became popular, and two of our three current rites of penance originate from this development. It seems that the monks had read how Jesus was liberal in forgiving people, in telling us to do likewise, and in not laying down any law that reconciliation with God and the community was a once-in-a-lifetime event. By the end of the eighth century, a manual for priests called *Penitentials* was produced. This manual gave advice on suitable penalties for various sins. From the ninth to the eleventh centuries, Western Christians became obsessed by their unworthiness to receive holy communion and of their great need for the forgiveness of their sins. In 1215, the church had to enact a law that remains with us today, requiring Catholics to receive communion at least once a year, at Eastertime. From then until Vatican II, this sacrament was often a trial, where the exact nature of sins, the number, variety, and gravity had to be carefully confessed by the penitent and weighed up by the priest. The more severe and public nature of the previous ritual was replaced by a private manifestation of one's conscience to Christ through the ministry of the priest. While the outcome for many walking away from confession may have been relief for some, and a freedom from shame and an ability to start again for others, it also encouraged a scrupulosity—a dread of sinning again, of being too imperfect, and of feeling interrogated by the priest—that has left scars for many Catholics. It takes very little to hear their horror stories. In one of the great liturgical ironies, Vatican II, while ushering in a return to the generous and merciful love of Jesus in the Gospels, moved the emphasis of this sacrament from confessing one's sins to being reconciled with God and our neighbors. It also saw a dramatic decline in people attending the sacrament. The reasons for this development are many, but once a God of fear and retribution was successfully replaced with one of mercy and compassion, the need for a private ritualized penitential ritual was less acutely needed by many.

The Example of Jesus

Don't tell some Catholics, but Jesus had next to nothing to say about sex. That doesn't mean it's not important. It is just a fact that he very rarely addressed himself to sexuality in either a positive or negative way. Maybe he knew some Catholic theologians weren't going to shut up about it for the next two thousand years! According to the Gospels, the two biggest sins Jesus returns to the most are lack of forgiveness and hypocrisy, where all of us at some point say one thing and do another. Indeed, it is easy to see how hypocrisy and lack of forgiveness are linked. Possibly the greatest betrayal, for Jesus, is telling others that they should forgive those who have hurt them, and then not practicing what they preach in the forgiveness of others.

At our Christian burial, can it be said, "Here we farewell a forgiving person"? As true followers of Jesus, of all the virtues we are meant to embody and live, forgiveness is clearly preeminent. In the Synoptic Gospels, we just need to recall the parable of the Good Samaritan (Luke 10:25–37); the Unmerciful Servant (Matt 18:23–35); the Widow and the Unjust Judge (Luke 18:1–8); the Pharisee and the Tax Collector (Luke 18:9–14); as well as Jesus, as part of the Lord's Prayer, teaching us that we should forgive as much as we have been forgiven by God (Matt 6:9–14; Luke 11:1–4); Jesus forgiving his false accusers (Luke 23:34); and the Eucharist as an act of reconciliation (Matt 26:28). No one ever promised us that living the Christian life was easy, and true forgiveness is among the hardest things we can ever do.

While in Luke's Gospel forgiveness runs through so much of the teaching and preaching of Jesus, it is in Luke 15 where it comes to the fore. This chapter has three of the great meditations on how merciful God is and, in turn, how we must also be. Here, the context for this chapter matters. In Luke 15, Jesus responds to charges about the company he was keeping and especially those with whom he dined. In Jesus's day, one only ate with intimates, and yet Jesus shared his table with notorious sinners. These three parables are given as an explanation for this practice: the lost sheep, the lost coin, and the lost son. In each case, the shepherd, the woman, and the father go to ridiculous lengths to save that which is lost.

In this light we can see why this chapter became so important to the earliest Christian theologians in talking about the sacrament of penance. As we have seen, who was admitted or readmitted to the eucharistic table was very important. These three parables reveal that the table of the Lord is here for those of us who know the frailty of our lives enough to recognize our hunger and thirst for Christ. Jesus didn't seem to care much about how and where we were lost, just that we knew he was searching for us, and that upon finding us were welcomed into his compassionate arms. This theology was eventually ritualized in this reconciling sacrament.

The Lost Sheep. A new, city-based bishop now appointed to a diocese in the outback of Australia, famous for its huge sheep ranches, was explaining to the confirmation class how he was the shepherd of the flock. Given that many of the children's families were involved in the sheep industry, he said that he was "like the Good Shepherd who cares for all the sheep." The students seemed consoled. Warming up, the bishop continued, "For instance, what would your father do if he lost one of his sheep?" The class was silent. The bishop asked again. The students were confused. The bishop got personal, "Michael, what would your dad do if he lost one of his sheep?" "Well, bishop, seeing Dad's got forty-two thousand of them, he'd let the bastard go!"

Sometimes the power of the gospel needs a little help to become inculturated. If the well-meaning bishop had done his homework and understood the economic unit that a sheep represented in first-century Palestine, he would have asked Michael about 420 missing sheep and gotten the answer he was seeking.

This parable is critical to our understanding of the sacrament of penance because sometimes when we want to return to the Lord and say sorry, we can think we have taken the initiative in seeking out God's mercy. In fact, the desire to seek forgiveness is already God's gift at work in us. Amazing grace is always the first mover. The Good Shepherd risks everything, even the safety of those who are presently okay, to seek and save the one who needs saving the most. The old story is told of the young atheist who cynically asked the priest, "Do you think I will ever find God?" to which the priest replied, "No, but I am sure God will find you—if you let him." None of us is coerced into Jesus's flock. We're not victims of the Good Shepherd. We choose to belong or we go along another path. But throughout our lives and through a myriad of people and ways, Jesus seeks us out so that we may find the way, the truth, and the life. The end of the parable is one of the great insights into the nature of God. Jesus says that God takes the ones that are lost into his arms and carries them home where he rejoices and celebrates. It is not by accident that the image of Jesus, the Good Shepherd, carrying the lamb home on his shoulders is among the oldest images of Jesus we have in Christian art. This sacrament sharpens our hearing to his call and helps us to delight in his embrace. And it calls us to do likewise: to risk everything to be foolishly loving and compassionate as we actively seek out those who most need to experience God's mercy and saving love.

The Lost Coin. Rejoicing occurs again at the end of the short parable about the woman who finds the lost coin. The original text says she lost one of ten drachmas. A drachma in the time of Jesus was equivalent to a day's wage, so while she could possibly survive on nine tenths of her income, the lost coin mattered in ways we could never know. Furthermore, Kenneth Bailey reminds us that "the peasant village is, to a considerable extent, self-supporting, making its own cloth and growing its own food. Cash is a rare commodity. Hence the lost coin is of far greater value in a peasant home than the day's labor it represents monetarily."[1]

Whatever its value to the woman, and in a windowless house, she risks the price of expensive oil and arduous work to find it. There are two ways to read this parable: the value of the coin to the owner and the security and comfort it brings, as well as seeing that some of us are the metaphorical lost coins. In this latter and rich reading of the story, God, who treasures us and knows our value, does everything possible, indeed exhaustively, to find us. Either way, though undeserved on our part, the result is that God rejoices with all and sundry in that he has been reconciled with the one who was lost.

The Lost Son. After the lost sheep and the lost coin, we read the most famous parable of all three, and arguably the New Testament: the lost son. Understandably, it has also been called "the parable of the prodigal son," "the lost sons," and "the forgiving father." By whatever name we give it, this parable is one of the greatest short stories ever told about the human condition. However, to appreciate it fully, we need context.

What is shocking about this lost son is that everything about the Jewish culture of first-century Palestine sets the boy up for a fall: he was greedy for his father's inheritance; we can assume he left the promised land for the far country, where he squandered his inheritance recklessly; he ended up eating with the unclean pigs; and then he had the temerity to return and ask for forgiveness. This was the least like-able kid in town. In his social context, he did *not* deserve to be treated better than a slave. That's what makes the boy's father so magnificent in love. He was derided by his faithful older son for this folly of the heart, and he would have been considered a fool by his neighbors. As Monica Hellwig states, "The emphasis in the teaching of Jesus was not on determination of guilt, but on invitation and empowerment to conversion and the life of the reign of God. In all the gospel scenes in which Jesus is shown in conversation with sinners, the point of the narrative is precisely that he does not want to dwell on the past because guilt is paralyzing, but directs attention to the future and the possibilities for change."[2]

The reaction of the older son is why the parable is sometimes named "the lost sons." The younger son had clearly lost his way in life, but the older son had lost his soul, his humanity. I have more than a little sympathy for the obedient, faithful, and hardworking elder brother. He witnessed his impetuous sibling mock their dad, claim the money, blow the lot on women in prostitution, and then return home. His instinct was to punish the kid. Most people can understand his resentment, but his condemnation of his brother is in stark contrast to his father's extraordinary love and justice. On this last point, it seems clear that the younger son is not going to get back his inheritance. He has already spent it. The remaining older son will inherit all that he justly deserves: "The father said to him, 'Son, you are always with me, and all that is mine is yours. But we had to celebrate and rejoice, because this brother of yours was dead and has come to life; he was lost and has been found'" (Luke 15:31–32). Justice demands that we are never cruel. We can stand up for our principles, apply them, hold people to account for the consequences of their actions, but not degrade or dehumanize them. The parable finishes with a cliffhanger; we never hear if the older son relents and rejoices with the father and his brother at the party. We assume so, and we hope the father's forgiveness and love recuses both sons. It would be heartbreaking for a dad to wait and watch for his boy to return from a distant land, and then, when he got him home, watch his older son journey to a remote place with anger and resentment as his only companions. Resentment is a poison we inject into ourselves.

On every level, the sacrament of penance takes us back to basics, to the base desires and actions of our humanity that sees us lose our way, and to the basic teachings and actions of Jesus that make sure we are never stranded in this desolate place. In Luke 15, we get a schema for how we should all live, for what the church should be like, and how this sacrament should be celebrated in Christ's name: enabling us to live beyond our histories and having the courage and faith to be ridiculously generous and magnificently loving in how we seek and search, find and forgive.

What Is Sin?

If we are called to be as forgiving to others as Christ is to us, then we need to understand what God liberates us from and what we are meant to forgive in others.

Before we look at the Bible, I have always found Seneca, a first-century Roman philosopher, to be helpful. Seneca wrote a famous book on anger and how to deal with it. As we discussed earlier, he noticed especially how his richest friends were the angriest of all, and he came to believe that the reason so many people were agitated was that they had an unreasonable expectation about how smoothly their day would go. Those who were rich thought that their money would buy them an easier life, and when it didn't, they got the angriest. He saw that not dealing with realistic and human expectations of our personal frailty and the vicissitudes of each day saw us live disordered lives, and that our anger was a sign of our sinfulness, of being out of kilter with who we truly are and the complexity of our lives. The world seems to be angrier than ever, and about all sorts of things, some of which are entirely justified. It's an interesting idea that this reflects our sinfulness, our alienation from ourselves and from God.

The concept of sin and of being forgiven and saved from sinfulness defines the religions of the Book (Judaism, Christianity, and Islam). In Genesis 2, we read the story of humanity's original parents, Adam and Eve, and how they offended God by eating of the fruit of the tree of knowledge to establish themselves as God, knowing good and evil. This triggers a series of events: loss of innocence, hiding from God; blaming each other for the action; the serpent being condemned as the embodiment of evil; women suffering in childbirth; and, later, Adam and Eve being expelled from Eden, the place of paradise. Adam and Eve's sin, here, becomes the trigger for the alienation it established between the perfect Creator and his imperfect and rebellious creatures, and God's subsequent lament and anger at humanity's fall into sinfulness.

Protestant theologian Peter Adam says he finds non-Christians surprisingly open to the idea of original sin. "They recognize that something is wrong in society, and it's hard to work out how we caused so much damage. Humans did it, not the dolphins, not the ants. I find non-Christians intrigued by a metaphysical explanation for what's wrong." Adam claims that original sin does not mean people are bad; they are fallible. "One of the most striking effects of sin is its ability to blind us to its presence—we can all see that in other people but it's much harder in ourselves. We focus too much on whether we have done wrong, and ignore the good things we should have done, and have not done, because of ignorance, nervousness, or lack of vision as to how we help and love others."[3]

It is important to note that there are serious reasons why we should not take a literal reading of Genesis. For example, God creates humanity with the freedom to choose, and then seems to get angry when that choice is exercised. Evil, as represented by the serpent, is created by God—a very problematic proposition for a truly and fully loving being—who also appears to invest the serpent with stronger powers of persuasion than he has. Having been set up for a fall, Adam and Eve are punished for their sin by being alienated from God, demonstrated by their roaming the earth. Subsequent presentations of God's wrath at our lack of fidelity can suggest that God is no better than we are—brooding and angry—since humanity was punished for a situation that it did not create, and which was the result of a bad choice when it was offered.

These days we now read the story of Adam and Eve and the fall as the Hebrews theologizing about how evil came into the world, why human beings are imperfect and sinful, and about our estrangement from God. Once the breach between heaven and earth had begun, the rest of the Old Testament could be fairly described as God wrestling with his chosen people to bring about a healing of the breach. Israel longs, hopes, and looks for the day when such a remarriage between heaven and earth can occur.

Indeed, this marriage metaphor reaches full expression in the opening chapters of the Book of Hosea:

> I will now allure her,
>> and bring her into the wilderness,
>> and speak tenderly to her.
> From there I will give her her vineyards,
>> and make the Valley of Achor a door of hope.
> There she shall respond as in the days of her youth,
>> as at the time when she came out of the land of Egypt.

(Hos 2:14–15)

As Adrian Lyons has observed, "What is extraordinary is that instances of infidelity came to be interpreted not as fatal wounds to a dream of innocence, but as preludes to an era in which divine forgiveness deals realistically with life as we live it."[4]

The rest of the Old Testament gives us two broad concepts for sinfulness: the first is of a transgression, literally "stepping across the boundaries or limits," of going off course or losing our way; the second definition is that of "missing the mark," of not hitting the target for which we were aiming or that which was rightly expected of us. Using either concept, it is God through the law and prophets who reveals what the limits or the marks are, and how we can account for ourselves. In the Old Testament, God takes transgressions of his law very seriously. At times, he rages at humanity's sinfulness and then, at other times, loves us enough to constantly forgive us and enables us to try again. Eventually, of course, for Christians, the law of love takes human form in Jesus Christ, and through his life we see in action how our own life should be lived.

The *Catechism* differentiates between two primary categories of sin: mortal sin and venial sin. Mortal sin is so serious that it means we reject eternal salvation by participating in it. It is a grave action committed freely, deliberately, and with full knowledge. Venial sin can be important but not deadly and needs to be avoided if we are going to live a joyous Christian life (*CCC* §§1854–64). Furthermore, the *Catechism* reminds us that we do not just commit personal sins but that we are also complicit in participating in unjust structures, and that we commit social sins when we engage in sexism, racism, genocide, and oppression of the poor (§1869).

Christian theologians have helpfully teased out how this relates to our daily lives. Anglican theologian Andrew McGowan says what's original about sin is its universality. "It's an insipid and inadequate view of humans to think we are all blank books and fine until someone comes along and stuffs things up for us. Selfishness and sin are almost synonymous."[5]

That's why, when we are baptized in Christ, we acknowledge both original sin and original grace. God's love comes alive in us even though we are aware of how far we stray from that love. Though we can do despicable things and make evil decisions, the Christian concept of sin is predicated on our theology of hope. The sacrament of penance rightly focuses on the gap between conscience and action, but only in the light of God's forgiveness made real in Jesus. William Uren observes, "It's about God's redeeming love that no matter how far away we seem there is a loving God who has reached out. The wages of sin doesn't have to be death. It's a revolutionary message. It means that in the vicissitudes of life, sin and failure aren't the end."[6]

I now understand why a spiritual director of mine, Fr. Ray O'Leary, used to encourage me to "take your eyes off the sinner and look to the Savior." Not that our sinfulness doesn't matter, but precisely because it *does* matter, and we can find a way out of it in Christ the Lord. "Let no one mourn that he [*sic*] has fallen again and again; for forgiveness has risen from the grave."[7] This explains in part why, in a world hellbent on revenge, resentment, and retribution, Pope Francis thought it was right for the church to have an Extraordinary Jubilee Year of Mercy. His intention was not just that believers would experience afresh the forgiveness of God, but that we would, in turn, be "compassionate as the Father is compassionate." Declaring this movement to be a jubilee was an act of great insight. As noted earlier, once in most people's lifetimes, Israel used to have a Year of Jubilee where three major things, among others, would happen: the slaves would be set free, the fields would go fallow, and the debts would be forgiven. These three themes mirror Francis's desire for the church: that we would liberate others by our compassion because we have been set free by God; that we would treat creation with respect and find our home within as its stewards not its wreckers; and that all this comes from knowing that God's forgiveness far outstrips our indebtedness.

What follows is just a sample of some of the things that Pope Francis said in the Year of Mercy that inspired me:

> "The time has come for the Church to take up the joyful
> call to mercy once more. It is time to return to the basics

and to bear the weaknesses and struggles of our brothers and sisters."

"If I had to sum it up in one word I would say that mercy is about being large-hearted. Our God is a large-hearted God."

"If up till now you have kept him at a distance, step forward. He will receive you with open arms."

"Jesus affirms that mercy is not only an action of the Father, it becomes a criterion for ascertaining who His true children are. In short, we are called to show mercy because mercy has first been shown to us."

"Pardoning offences becomes the clearest expression of merciful love, and for us Christians it is an imperative from which we cannot excuse ourselves."

"To become saints only one thing is necessary: to accept the grace that the Father gives us in Jesus Christ. There, this grace changes our heart. We continue to be sinners for we are weak, but with this grace which makes us feel that the Lord is good, that the Lord is merciful, that the Lord waits for us, that the Lord pardons us, this immense grace that changes our heart."

"I think we too are the people who, on the one hand, want to listen to Jesus, but on the other hand, at times, like to find a stick to beat others with, to condemn others. And Jesus has this message for us: mercy.... This is the Lord's most powerful message: mercy."

"We must never, never allow the throwaway culture to enter our hearts!...No one is disposable!"

Everything the pope says about God's mercy is an articulation of the best approaches to the sacrament of penance, for this is the liturgical moment where we seek, claim, and celebrate that there is nothing we have ever done for which God's mercy is not greater. There is no doubt, because he has said so, that the first and primary source of Pope Francis's great love for God is that he is much forgiven. The secondary source is St. Ignatius Loyola, the founder of the Jesuits, the religious order to which he belongs.

Resisting Sin

St. Ignatius Loyola's reflections on forgiveness and mercy were borne out of bitter, firsthand experiences where, in the cave at Manresa in 1522, his penances became so compulsive and obsessive that they did not lead him to God but were dangerous symptoms of self-destruction. St. Ignatius came to see that when we habitually sin, it doesn't "just happen." Sometimes, people may say, "I fly off the handle, but it comes out of nowhere"; "I have a problem with alcohol (or drugs, gambling, eating, working, stealing, sexual dysfunction, pornography, being violent at home, or any type of obsessive compulsive behavior, for example, hoarding or shopping) and I don't know where it comes from." St. Ignatius realized that our destructive behavior has a history, a pattern, and a story. It never just happens. He developed *The Examen* so that at least once a day, and preferably twice, we would stop and consider the moments in the day when we felt closest to God and the ones where we felt the most distant. The goal was not just the daily review, but more importantly, that over time we would come to see the patterns of those choices that lead us to life and consolation, and those that are destructive and lead to desolation.

In *The Examen*, we talk to Jesus as we would to our very best friend. It is best to do it around noon and then again at night, but at least at night. There are six simple steps:

1. Be still and become aware of the presence of God.
2. Review the day gently and with gratitude. Walk through the day and note its joys and delights.
3. Pay attention to how we felt in the day: where was the

light and the good moments? Were we alone or with others, in a special setting or an ordinary one? How did it leave us feeling?

4. Now look calmly at where the dark and the desolate moments occurred. Were we alone or with others, in a special or ordinary setting? How did it leave us feeling? Ask for forgiveness, if necessary.

5. Choose one feature of the day and ask the Holy Spirit to help us learn from it. Seek God's protection and help and seek his wisdom in making better choices.

6. Look toward tomorrow and ask God's help to learn what we can from today and to make decisions for tomorrow so that we might have more lightness and less darkness.

The process is not simply about looking at the events of the day but rather at the patterns that emerge over time. Ignatius believed that there is always a pattern to what gives us life and to our destructive behavior. Things never "just happen." Capitalize on the former and stare down and limit the damage of the latter.

The thing I like best about *The Examen* is that it is proactive. This process alerts us to the fact that the best pathway to forgiveness is not being passive, but being active, becoming aware, and dealing with the patterns of our downfall, while capitalizing on the choices that lead to life. There is little point in being sorry for the consequences of our sinfulness and yet not changing the pattern of behavior that leads us to ruin each time.

The secular world's insightful spin on *The Examen* is the twelve-step program of Alcoholics Anonymous that enshrines similar wisdom for people who may find the leap of faith a step too far. Steps four to ten confirm that you:

Step 1. We admitted we were powerless over alcohol—that our lives had become unmanageable.

Step 2. Came to believe that a Power greater than ourselves could restore us to sanity.

Step 3. Made a decision to turn our will and our lives over to the care of God *as we understood Him*.

Step 4. Made a searching and fearless moral inventory of ourselves.

Step 5. Admitted to God, to ourselves, and to another human being the exact nature of our wrongs.

Step 6. Were entirely ready to have God remove all these defects of character.

Step 7. Humbly asked Him to remove our shortcomings.

Step 8. Made a list of all persons we had harmed, and became willing to make amends to them all.

Step 9. Made direct amends to such people wherever possible, except when to do so would injure them or others.

Step 10. Continued to take personal inventory and when we were wrong promptly admitted it.

Step 11. Sought through prayer and meditation to improve our conscious contact with God *as we understood Him*, praying only for knowledge of His will for us and the power to carry that out.

Step 12. Having had a spiritual awakening as the result of these steps, we tried to carry this message to alcoholics, and to practice these principles in all our affairs.

No matter what we have ever done, we are greater than our worst moments. In the sacrament of penance, Christ does not condemn us, but offers grace and mercy so that we not only experience his forgiveness here and now, but are enabled to make the best choices so that we can stare down the destructive elements within ourselves and choose life.

Like a Seal on Your Heart

No doubt the "seal of the confession" has always fired the imagination of many: What do priests hear in there? What do they remember? How does it weigh on their consciences? These questions certainly became lively ones after the Catholic Alfred Hitchcock's film noir masterpiece, *I Confess*, of 1953. In it, Fr. Logan hears the confession of a husband regarding how he killed his wife that was, in fact, a pretext to framing the priest for the crime. Fr. Logan is put on trial for murder but will not divulge the information that will set him free. For the rest of the story you need to watch the film! This taut drama started endless discussions on the duties and obligations of a penitent and a priest; and endless "what if" scenarios regarding the sacrament of penance.

Because we have seen a dramatic decline in the numbers of Catholics in the developed world attending confession in recent decades, the discussions about the seal have been few. This was all true until the clergy sexual abuse of children scandal broke across the developed world. Given the Catholic Church's appalling record in covering up cases of sexual abuse of minors by church personnel, there is now much discussion about what a priest might have heard, especially from another priest, and very strongly held views about his legal obligations, especially in increasingly secular societies, to protect children from harm. When the public comes up against canon law, the protection of even one child wins every time.

Although it is changing quickly in many countries, there are only four vocations whose professional disclosures are currently protected as "confidential" by the courts: lawyers, psychiatrists, journalists, and priests in the role of hearing confession. Medical doctors used to be covered, but now many nations oblige all medicos to report mandatorily any child sexual abuse they encounter or suspect. Priests are only covered if the information they hear is obtained during confession. The reason why the law has, until now, protected the nature of specific conversations with lawyers, psychiatrists, and priests is the following: if a person is to be defended, then the lawyer needs to know the truth, even if some of the truth they hear is criminal—they need the whole story; if a psychiatrist is to enable a person to recover from a mental illness, it is essential the patient's history and exact nature of their experience be explored; and if a penitent is to repent, then he or she needs to be able to tell the truth freely. For the sake of transparency and spiritual health, the priest may need to hear about actions that, in ordinary situations, he would prefer not to be privy to.

In all three cases, the obligation of legal reporting would cut across what defense, care, and counsel may be offered. If we are as passionate about child protection as we should be, then the case for a change to mandatory reporting for clergy should be equally applied to the other two professions as well. I cannot see how or why we could make any exceptions. While all of us consider the sexual abuse of a child as a particularly heinous crime, if that despicable action is one that demands mandatory reporting to the police, then, while I am generally suspicious of slippery slope arguments, if we criminalize the priest who hears about the sexual abuse of children, a similar and valid argument could be made for priests to report any criminal activity they hear in the confessional. This would include illegal drug use, any type of theft, any physical or sexual abuse of adults, especially rape in marriage, some forms of pornography, avoidance of taxation, software piracy, hastening death or assisting a suicide, and even the failure of anyone to report a crime to the police. It was not long ago that it would have also meant reporting a woman who had an abortion. Currently in many developing countries, it would also mean Catholic priests would have to report adultery and homosexuality. However, as vigilant as we must be about the sexual safety of minors, the greater good might be better served if abusive clients, patients, and penitents can tell their story without the threat of mandatory reporting. If the civil law in regard to the seal of confession changes, and priests are sent to jail for what it is alleged they heard in the confessional (I can also imagine there may be some hostile people who could set up a priest or a bishop in this regard to prove a point against an individual they do not like, or against the church because of its nondisclosure principle), some priests might stop hearing confessions altogether for fear of their civil and legal exposure, or others might publicize that they will not hear confessions that involve child sexual abuse. This would be the same process as some counselors, psychotherapists, and psychologists do now in stating the cases to which they do not attend.

Penance

It is said that Jesuits like distinctions to the point of distraction, but several distinctions really matter in the debate about the absolute seal of secrecy regarding the sacrament of penance. The first is that, while priests can never divulge what they hear in any confession that might lead to the identification of the penitent, they can speak generally about cases they have heard. This is necessary when a priest needs to check out with another priest or a professional about whether they gave the best advice. In all my years as a priest, I have never heard a case involving anyone who has abused a child. I don't doubt for a moment that it has happened, but in recent years, I have asked hundreds of other priests and no one has admitted to hearing such a confession. So at the very least, it is such a rare event (except in the public's imagination) that the old dictum might apply: "extreme cases don't prove principles." Not that this in any way takes away from the potential of what could be said in the confessional and the horrible implications for the conscience of the priest who hears it, just that, during most confessions, child sexual abuse is not mentioned.

From the studies on the psychiatric profiles of pedophiles, we know they thrive on keeping their activities secret. They almost always demand secrecy from their victims by threats or inducements. They appear to be expert in grooming victims in families and institutional settings whom they know they can intimidate to keep quiet. Thank God that victims and survivors have broken their silence and have now come forward about what happened to them in the family home, at the hands of clergy, or in other institutional settings. So while the veil of secrecy in the confessional may seem that the church is accommodating actions of a child abuser, it would be extremely rare for such a person who needs silence to carry out such evil actions to take the risk of telling anyone about what he has done.

We also know that pedophiles lead psychologically compartmentalized lives. While some people may think that the perpetrators need to repent of their crimes to function, psychological and family studies tell us that perpetrators do not process their actions in the ordinary way. First, as difficult as it is to accept, such criminals can abuse children and carry on with their daily lives as though no crime had ever been committed. However, given that it is still required for a person to have the option to go to confession anonymously, if a priest, in this situation, is subject to mandatory reporting, does he ask for his name and number and call the police? Does he guess his identity? Does he call the police and tell them what someone whom he can't identify came and confessed? At best, the priest is obliged to identify both perpetrator and the victim.

Second, while it is possible for someone to confess the sin of child sexual abuse, it does not mean that they are forgiven. To fulfill all the obligations of the sacrament, a person must do their penance. In the unlikely event that I would hear the confession of a sexual abuser, I would argue to the penitent that, if he or she is sincerely sorry for the heinous crime they have committed, we should go to the police immediately, right there and then. While under the present law of the church (cann. 220 and 960), I cannot make going to the police a penance for this or any other moral crime. However, I can advise him that this is the best course of action. Perhaps these two laws need to be changed so that, if this penance is not done, then it would be clear there is no absolution. While this would not be foolproof, I doubt that anyone genuinely coming to the sacrament of penance and confessing this egregious sin without any desire to take responsibility for what they have done to their victim would accompany me to the authorities. There are other examples of when the penance may be directly related to the crime. In the cases of significant theft, a penance and absolution would usually be connected to the restitution of the money or goods that have been stolen. And, especially if someone else has been convicted and punished for a crime to which the penitent now confesses, penance and absolution would be connected to owning up to the authorities so that the wrongly convicted person can be set free.

Third, for a priest to be obliged by the seal of confession, all the obligations of the sacrament must be in place. The penitent must approach me to participate in the formal ritual of the sacrament of penance that is clearly distinguished from having a chat. If it is the latter, then I am bound to report to the police what I have heard in that casual conversation. This is presently the case in every developed country in the world that priests must always abide by.

A gray area exists in hearing the confession of someone who was abused as a child by any adult. Jesuit moral philosopher Bill Uren sums up the situation:

> The sole subject of the seal of confession are the sins of the penitent and only those other circumstances which are integral to the nature of the sin. So, if a small child comes to the sacrament of reconciliation and says she has been sexually abused by her uncle, precisely because it is not her sin it does *not* fall under the seal of confession. She is not the sinning perpetrator or accomplice, she is the innocent victim of the abuse. The priest would not be breaking the seal if he reported such an incident to the police. Because of the common misunderstanding that everything that happens in the confessional falls under the seal of confession, the priest would probably be well advised to ask the child to repeat outside the confessional what she has said inside the confessional. But whether said inside or outside the confessional, the report that one has been the victim of sexual abuse does not fall under the seal of confession. Of course, if there are matters other than sin that are revealed in the confessional, they would also normally be regarded as strictly confidential.[8]

It can be argued that what applies to a child applies to an adult as well. I do, however, also need to state that there are several canon lawyers who hold that the confessional is so sacred that everything said there is protected and that any disclosure of the sin and of the sinner is punishable with automatic excommunication. The Vatican has not finally expressed a view on this question. In all cases, therefore, great sensitivity is required.

Since the church does not deserve the benefit of the doubt in the public domain because of a scandalous cover-up of the criminal behavior of a very small number of its personnel, the greater pastoral good for the greatest number still flows from the confidence with which a genuinely repentant person can approach the sacrament of penance. In our heightened desire to see everyone everywhere take child protection very seriously, we can cut across what can be a genuinely pastoral relationship in the sacrament of penance that might see people who have committed a serious crime repent of their sin with genuine sorrow and admit their crime to civil authorities so as to give their victim some justice and healing. Given how rarely this crime is confessed, then, along with lawyers and psychiatrists, society's gamble on protecting such disclosures from these three professions is worthwhile so that these professionals can work with the abuser to let justice prevail.

The Mission to Forgive

It may not come as any surprise that a Jesuit writer selects *The Mission* as a contemporary parable on the sacrament of penance. It is one of the best films to demonstrate that interior battles are as important as exterior ones and that the two can be closely connected.

In eighteenth-century Paraguay, Spanish Jesuits left the settled towns for the "land above the falls." These journeys were unsuccessful because the people of that land were wary of the colonizers, who sought to sell them as slaves. At the end of the treacherous journey beyond the waterfall, Jesuit missionaries were martyred for their trouble. Yet, armed only with his Bible and oboe, Fr. Gabriel decides to make the journey himself. Captured by the Guarani people, he plays music for them and they are entranced. The mission above the falls begins.

Later, Gabriel witnesses the handiwork of slave traders led by Captain Rodrigo Mendoza. Gabriel visits him and suggests that he should repent of his sins. Mendoza insists that no penance is great enough to cover them all. Gabriel assures him there is: "Do you dare try it?" And thus Mendoza is drafted into the service of the mission.

The Jesuits find themselves caught between the papal envoy and the colonizers in a fight for the rights of the native people. The envoy brings orders to close the mission. Gabriel resists the idea that the church must bow to political realities. He adds, "If might is right, then love has no place in the world."

The story of the mission is based on history, though we have no record of a former slave trader/mercenary who became a Jesuit novice called Mendoza (Robert De Niro) or otherwise, or a superior called Fr. Gabriel (Jeremy Irons). However, in 1493, Pope Alexander VI divided the world between the two great superpowers of the day: Portugal and Spain. This arrangement worked well until the riches of South America were discovered and claimed by both countries. Rome was called on to settle disputes between the two. Through the Treaty of Madrid in 1750, an exchange of land took place. The transition of authority was bloody. The Guarani were defeated in 1758. The pope suppressed the Jesuits in 1773.

In 1987, this film won the Palm D'Or at Cannes, the Golden Lion at Venice, and the Silver Bear at Berlin. It also won an Academy Award that year for Best Cinematography, beaten for Best Picture by *Platoon*.

For our discussion, let's focus on Rodrigo Mendoza, who makes his living kidnapping natives from the Guarani community and selling them to nearby plantations. After returning from another kidnapping trip, Mendoza is told by his fiancée that she loves his younger half brother, Felipe. Mendoza later finds them in bed together and, in a fit of rage, kills Felipe in a duel. Although he is acquitted of the killing, Mendoza spirals into depression and seeks absolution for his actions. Fr. Gabriel visits him in his cell as he slowly starves himself to death and challenges Mendoza to undertake a suitable penance by accompanying the Jesuits on their return to the Guarani community above the falls and to ask the people he enslaved to forgive him. He accepts but decides to do extra penance by dragging a very heavy bundle containing the armor and swords that he used as a slave trader. Against the protests of the accompanying Jesuits, Mendoza carries his burden until he comes face-to-face with the only people he feels who can release him from his crimes and the burden of shame, guilt, and sin. His journey to this meeting and the meeting itself are examples of the power of forgiveness in and through this sacrament. Everything Mendoza desires and hopes for from the Guarani we desire and hope for from God.

The Mission is predicated on three theological principles: the importance of repentance, which leads to the freedom found in forgiveness; the mission of Christians to love (at one stage Fr. Gabriel says, "If might is right, then love has no place in the world. I don't have the strength to live in such a world"); and discerning the action of the Holy Spirit so that we can trust the promptings of our informed consciences—recalling that Blessed John Henry Newman called conscience "the aboriginal Vicar of Christ."[9] This last point cannot be overemphasized when we come to penance. Sometimes we can spend so much time dealing with the consequences of what we have chosen and who we have become that we don't give sufficient time and energy to attending to how we might avoid sin and destruction in the first place.

Discerning from a position of being in love is superbly summarized in one of my favorite quotes attributed to Pedro Arrupe, SJ:

> Nothing is more practical than finding God, that is, than falling in love in a quite absolute, final way. What you are in love with, what seizes your imagination, will affect everything. It will decide what will get you out of bed in the morning, what you do with your evenings, how you spend your weekends, what you read, who you know, what breaks your heart, and what amazes you with joy and gratitude. Fall in love, stay in love, and it will decide everything.[10]

5

Holy Orders

Priesthood of All Believers

IN MOST INSTITUTIONS, the official leadership group constitutes a fraction of the organization, but almost always, and for good reasons, the focus on them is disproportionate to their membership. This is certainly true of the Catholic Church. While figures are debatable, it is estimated that there are 1.25 billion Catholics in the world. Figures for those men who have been ordained as bishops, priests, and deacons are much more reliable. The last Vatican census concluded that there are 5,067 bishops (active and retired), 414,300 priests, and 43,195 permanent deacons. This means that 462,575 men have been ordained to one or all three of the orders of service in the church. Though professed men and women religious are among our greatest leaders, these unordained leaders number 54,229 men and 670,320 women. This means that ordained members of the church constitute just 0.037 percent of the body, and even when we add in the religious who have not been ordained, they make up only 0.094 percent of the entire community.

These numbers tell some of the story. The most important sacrament of Christian leadership is not holy orders but baptism. As with every other sacrament, if there is no baptism, there can be no holy orders. As important as good leaders are in every community, the sacramental priesthood granted in holy orders is a flourishing of the priesthood of all believers given at baptism. "The anointing with sacred chrism… signifies the gift of the Holy Spirit to the newly baptized, who has become a Christian, that is, one 'anointed' by the Holy Spirit, incorporated into Christ who is anointed priest, prophet, and king" (*CCC* §1241), to "become living stones to be built into a spiritual house, to be a holy priesthood.…By Baptism they share in the priesthood of Christ, in his prophetic and royal mission.…Baptism gives a share in the common priesthood of all believers" (*CCC* §1268).

So baptism is fundamental in understanding Christian priesthood, but this theological reality has been obscured for too long and at too high a price. "The concept of the 'priesthood of all believers' entails an understanding of ministry as something which is not exclusive to bishops, priests, and deacons. We are all called to ministry; the role of bringing the gospel of Jesus to our world, evangelizing, and being servants of that Good News. This is a role that each person in the body of Christ must fulfill. This has affected our ideas about the role and exercise of the ordained ministry. The ordained priesthood is seen as one aspect, albeit an important one, of the common priesthood."[1]

Ordination and Leadership

There is an important distinction to be made between ordination and leadership, though it is important to keep this distinction in perspective. While ordination gives a deacon, priest, or bishop sacramental and structural power, it does not necessarily bestow upon him the gift of leadership, which can only be granted by followers. There are some priests who may be ordained, but they are not leading anyone anywhere. There are women and men who have never and will never be ordained, but their leadership is inspiring. If we look beyond sacramental leadership—a central reality of the Catholic Church's life—and examine education, healthcare, welfare, pastoral care, and spirituality, we find that in almost every Western country in the world, the priesthood of all believers is indispensable to our mission in the world. In fact, if they stopped leading and working in all these ministries, the daily work of the church would come to a halt. It might be a good thing if the lay faithful of the church, especially women, went on strike one week to remind the ordained men who is actually running this "show" in and through their sometimes heroic, self-sacrificing service.

Similarly, it is important that we recognize the equal dignity of women and men created in the image and likeness of God and their complementarity and mutuality, so that it translates into the active participation of women and men throughout all levels of decision-making in the church, a reexamination of the nature of nonpriestly ministry with the exploration of more inclusive roles for men and women, and a reform of practices that do not promote the equality of men and women.

Pope Francis has initiated a discussion on the role of women in the life of the church. "Demands that the legitimate rights of women be respected, based on the firm conviction that men and women are equal in dignity, present the church with profound and challenging questions which cannot be lightly evaded....This presents a great challenge for pastors and theologians, who are in a position to recognize more fully what this entails with regard to the possible role of women in decision-making in different areas of the Church's life" (*Evangelii Gaudium* 104). Later in this chapter, we will address directly women's exclusion from holy orders in the Catholic Church.

Weak Enough to Be Ordained?

In 1972, Fr. Michael Buckley, SJ, asked an ordination class not if they were strong enough to be ordained, but if they were weak enough. He was not referring to the experience of sin, but "if weakness [is] at the heart of your lives....Weakness allows us to feel...the human struggle and darkness and anguish which calls out for salvation...[and] relates us profoundly with God, because it provides the arena in which his power can move and reveal itself (cf. 2 Cor 12:9–10)." Although I did not know it when I read that essay, my own ordination as a priest was a sign of other vulnerabilities wherein the power of amazing grace can be manifest.

I was ordained a priest at the Jesuit parish of North Sydney on December 11, 1993. I was ordained with a good friend and now acclaimed writer, Michael McGirr. I was supposed to be ordained in Brisbane, the capital of my home state, but for a variety of Jesuit reasons, I was asked to join Michael in Sydney. Despite being friends, I can remember being very anxious as I rang him with this suggestion, imagining he may prefer to be ordained on his own, in his home parish, where his family had been pillars of the parish for generations. After a pause in the conversation, which I mistakenly took to be displeasure, he said, "Well Dickie" (Michael is one of the few people who can get away with calling me that) "this is a huge relief. You're more interested in liturgy than I am, so why don't we agree that you organize the ceremony and I'll just turn up." It didn't quite work out like that, but it did move in that direction.

Jesuit composer Christopher Willcock and I called in a few musician friends to help. We put together a seventy-voice choir, the brass and timpani from the Sydney Symphony Orchestra, and soloists from Opera Australia. As you can imagine, it was a very simple, low-key event!

In planning the ordination, I missed two things. The first was that that summer night was one of the hottest and most humid days anyone could remember. The temperature got to 100 degrees (38 Celsius). When the ceremony started at 8 p.m. it was still 81 degrees (27 Celsius). The second thing I missed in the planning was that that night, directly across the road from the church on the North Sydney Oval, the Salvation Army was conducting "Carols by Candlelight." It also started at 8 p.m. As the procession outside snaked its way to the back of the church and up the stairs to the entrance, all we could hear from the loud speakers booming across the road was "I'm dreaming of a white Christmas . . . ." It was so hot, I was too!

Michael and I had eight hundred of our closest family and friends packed into this non-air-conditioned church. The competition from the Salvos, however, meant that the people at the back couldn't hear very well. In fact, instead of the ceremony, all they could hear was "Jingle bells, jingle bells, jingle all the way…." So, what did people do? They closed the windows and doors. Observing this happen from the sanctuary was one thing, but then we felt a wave of heat roll up the church. I became more than a little nervous, as under the lights and the vestments the sanctuary became like a sauna.

During the singing of Fr. Willcock's splendid "Gloria," I began not feeling very well and sat down. Then I really started not feeling very well and went to put my head between my legs—the pose I wanted to strike at my ordination. As I did, I passed out on the floor.

Now, videos are wonderful things! This one showed that, as I sat down, my mother got out of the front pew, walked up on the sanctuary, and was there in time to catch me as I fell. I fell into my mother's arms. I have always thought that Sigmund Freud would have a field day with this moment—widowed mother catches celibate priest son at his ordination: Oedipus eat your heart out! My mother loves that part of the video because not only does it capture her doing what she calls her "Pieta trick," but because, as she explains, "That was the most expensive dress I have ever purchased in my life, and look, it fell beautifully on the floor. That dress was worth every cent I paid for it!"

I discovered that night that nothing stops a Fr. Christopher Willcock "Gloria." When I asked him later what he would've done if I had died, he laughed and said, "I would have said ladies and gentlemen of the choir and the band, please turn to the Requiem Mass at the back."

Once the "Gloria" had concluded, the bishop who, for good measure, was presiding at his first ever ordination, asked if there was a doctor in the congregation. This was a Jesuit ordination, so I was soon surrounded by a team of twelve medicos and a couple of nurses. I could have had every part of my anatomy dealt with by a specialist. It was just a heavy faint, but when I came to, the bishop wondered aloud what to do next. My then provincial, Fr. Bill Uren, SJ, told the bishop, "Well, we're not coming back tomorrow." And with that, Michael was dispatched to take me to the sacristy to have a walk around and a drink and to return when I was ready. When we got to the sacristy, I plaintively said to Michael, "I'm so sorry, Mick, I've ruined our ordination." "Don't be sorry, Dickie," he replied, "I'm not nervous at all now because I can't do anything more to muck this liturgy up than what you've already done."

Meanwhile, what was happening in the church was a study in human nature. Because my father died of a stroke at the age of thirty-six, I knew my immediate and extended family would be anxious that a serious episode had occurred. On the other side of the aisle, the McGirrs were understandably saying, "That Richard Leonard is such a show-off! It was our Michael's night, and now the focus is all on him." Across the aisle, my side was filling in the McGirr side about our family's medical history. So much so that, when Michael and I emerged from the sacristy, you could swear that Lazarus had just come out of the tomb. After the mandatory canonical questions were asked and before we proceeded, I knew that for my family's sake it was important that I say a few words so that they could be relieved that I had not suffered a stroke. The bishop agreed. I told the congregation, "You've just seen a perfectly planned liturgy go completely down the gurgler. So, we better just get on with it." And the crowd burst into supportive applause all over again.

Later that night, a Jesuit theologian told me, "This was the best ordination I have ever attended." I was curious, given that the style of music and liturgy that night would not have been to his taste. He tends to be a Kumbaya-My-Lord-on-a-bad-guitar kinda guy. "I don't know if you noticed," I replied, "but I passed out during the Gloria." "Yes, that's what made it really great." "How's that?" "Well," he went on excitedly, "as we were processing in singing Chris's glorious arrangement of 'All Creatures of our God and King,' you could not help but be filled with how great God is. And then, within a brief time, you have collapsed on the floor. It acted out the central drama of every liturgy: that God is great, and we are frail. That God looks on us in our frailty and sent Christ to sustain and support us in and through the Church. We come to public prayer because in our frailty we need God's grace to help us witness to the gospel. That's what made this the best ordination I have ever attended."

94

Some people have asked me whether I am embarrassed about passing out at my ordination ceremony. Why would I be? It provided me with the most valuable lesson about the sacrament of holy orders: God is great and we are frail, and if we know that shared human weakness is at the heart of our lives, we can be one with all those who need saving and so discover that the love of God can do infinitely more than we can hope or imagine as we witness to Christ in the world.

All Christian Leadership Imitates Christ

I like the mock management process about electing a world leader. Here are the facts about the three leading candidates:

Candidate A associates with crooked politicians, consults with astrologers, has had two mistresses, is severely disabled, chain smokes, and drinks eight to ten martinis a day.

Candidate B was kicked out of office twice, can easily sleep until noon, used opium at university, is an undiagnosed manic-depressive, and drinks a bottle of whiskey every day.

Candidate C is a decorated war hero, vegetarian, doesn't smoke or drink, except for an occasional beer. Though never married, he has never cheated on his common-law wife.

Who would you choose?

Candidate A is Franklin D. Roosevelt

Candidate B is Winston Churchill

Candidate C is Adolph Hitler

Sometimes the best candidate on paper is, in fact, the worst leader. Thank goodness Jesus did not hire a management consultancy to help him recruit his earliest disciples. On paper, Peter, James, and John would not have gotten past expressing interest in the job. Jesus recognized, however, that they had the three things necessary for Christian leadership: faith, hope, and love. Not that they had it immediately. We know they constantly misunderstood Jesus and tried to steer him in other ways, they made promises they did not keep, and abandoned Jesus when the going got tough. Nevertheless, they had the one thing that nearly all great leaders have in their formation: a mentor who knows they are not perfect, forgives their limitations, tells them the truth, helps them keep focused on what they are about, and inspires them by what he says and how he lives.

All leadership in the Christian Church is meant to imitate and follow on from the example of Jesus's leadership. Jesus was not monarchical or tyrannical. Without question, the most central element in the way Jesus led his followers was as their *servant*, of being the least. Following on from this, the Second Vatican Council taught that those in holy orders should be outstanding in three things: humility, charity, and simplicity of lifestyle. Some ordained leaders exemplify these virtues. Others, including me, have domesticated the hard edge of the gospel and have some way to go in understanding the call to radical servant leadership.

From the moment of Jesus's baptism to his resurrection, he did not demand submission or subjection from his followers as a worldly ruler of his day would have, but he loved them enough to serve them, and inspired them enough to do the same for others. His language toward his followers was a dramatic departure from the usual profile of the rabbi/student. Jesus called his disciples his friends. He spoke about his leadership as being like that of a shepherd—the Aramaic word he would have used for sheep is the same word used for servant. Hence, the Good Shepherd is prepared to die in service of his fellow servants. To be ordained into holy orders means a man must mirror the sacrificial love of Christ for the people of God so much that he is prepared to pay something, maybe everything, in serving them.

The second central element of Jesus's leadership was *obedience*, which comes from the Latin meaning "to give ear," "to listen attentively." The word *audio* comes from it too. This meaning reveals a new way of understanding Christ's obedience to the Father and our obedience to Christ. It does not have to be slavishly following another's will. Rather, to listen attentively is much more dynamic and mutual; it is about seeking understanding and knowing something so well, so intimately, that our will follows naturally our instincts, along with the humility to trust. Jesus made very clear, and St. Paul amplified it, that a Christian's primary obedience always and everywhere, as a leader or as a follower, is to Christ's law of love.

The third central element of Jesus's leadership was the simple and direct way he articulated and lived his vision of the *reign of God* in the world. This is clearly evidenced in the Gospel of Luke. At the very beginning of Jesus's public ministry, Luke summarizes what is called the program:

> Then Jesus, filled with the power of the Spirit, returned to Galilee, and a report about him spread through all the surrounding country. He began to teach in their synagogues and was praised by everyone.
>
> When he came to Nazareth, where he had been brought up, he went to the synagogue on the sabbath day, as was his custom. He stood up to read, and the scroll of the prophet Isaiah was given to him. He unrolled the scroll and found the place where it was written:
> "The Spirit of the Lord is upon me,
>   because he has anointed me
>   to bring good news to the poor.
> He has sent me to proclaim release to the captives
>   and recovery of sight to the blind,
>   to let the oppressed go free,
> to proclaim the year of the Lord's favor."
> And he rolled up the scroll, gave it back to the attendant, and sat down. The eyes of all in the synagogue were fixed on him. (4:14–20)

In the tradition of the greatest of the prophets, and now as the embodiment of their prophecies, Jesus has come for those of us who are poor, captive, blind, and oppressed. But unlike the former prophets, Jesus is not only a companion in our distress or an advocate on our behalf, he has also come to turn the world upside down and establish the definitive reign of God in our lives. In Jesus, all that Israel longed to see is fulfilled. So it follows that those in holy orders embody and lead the community by being companions to the poor, setting prisoners free, fighting oppression, enabling others to confront what they would prefer to ignore, and proclaiming boldly that there is no one beyond God's favor. Given the direct way Jesus outlined his program, for anyone called to ordination, these commissions are not optional extras. They define who a Christian leader is and how he or she is sent to lead others in changing the world.

The fourth element of Jesus's leadership was his *empowerment* of others to turn their own lives around, especially those who were least expected to respond to his call. While the earliest disciples would have struggled to pass anyone's criteria for leadership, our tradition holds that they all went on to spread the good news throughout the known world and die a martyr's death for Christ. The following tongue-in-cheek consultant's summary on those who had applied to lead the earliest Christian Church proves the point of Jesus seeing beyond the surface:

JOHN: Says he is a Baptist, but certainly doesn't dress like one. Has slept in the outdoors for months on end, has a weird diet, and picks fights in public with religious leaders.

PETER: Has a bad temper, has even been known to curse. Had a big run-in with Paul in Antioch. Aggressive. A loose cannon.

PAUL: Powerful, CEO type of leader and fascinating preacher. However, short on tact, unforgiving with young ministers, harsh, and has been known to preach all night.

JUDAS: His references are solid. Conservative. Good connections. Knows how to handle money. Great possibilities here.

Indeed, the same report says of Jesus:

> JESUS: Has been popular at times, but once, when his following grew to five thousand, he managed to offend them all and it dwindled down to some faithful women and his best friend. Seldom stays in one place very long.

From shepherds, eastern astrologers, pharisees, tax collectors, fishermen, centurions, zealots, notorious sinners, people with bad reputations, and even to people possessed with demons, Jesus called people who had, to say the least, complex backgrounds. He explicitly called sinners, those who did not fulfill the strict religious structures of their day. So it is clear that imitating such confidence and insight, those who lead today in Christ's name should call and empower not just those who may be well versed in virtue, but God's loved sinners who are called to be set free from the destructive behavior that might mark their lives, and, transformed by amazing grace, called to offer their talents and gifts for the kingdom as well.

The fifth element of Jesus's leadership was that he *confronted evil* and faced up to the consequences of how he lived—calling for justice, peace, compassion, and love of all. We do not believe that the Word of God became one with us as a human being simply and only to die. Rather, Jesus came to live, and because of the courageous and radical way he lived his life and the saving love he embodied for all humanity, he threatened the political, social, and religious authorities of his day so much that they executed him. This is an easier way for us to make sense of the predictions of the passion. Jesus was not clairvoyant; he was a full and true human being, and therefore, had informed but limited knowledge. His full and true divinity cannot obliterate his humanity or he would be playacting at being human. His divinity is seen in and through the uncompromisingly loving, just, and sacrificial way he lived within the bounds of his humanity. Jesus did not seek death for its own sake, but he would not and could not live any other way than faithfully, hopefully, and lovingly. In his day, as today, this is immensely threatening to those whose power base is built on values opposed to these virtues. The world continues to silence and sideline people who live out the Christian virtues and values now, just as Jesus was thought to be ultimately sidelined in his crucifixion. But God had the last word on the death of Jesus: *Life*.

So, to those who are in holy orders, we are called to be morally courageous people who follow in the tradition of the martyrs, not looking for death in any active sense but being prepared to die as a result of witnessing to faith in Christ and demanding the justice that must flow from it. With and in Christ we confront evil, death, and destruction head-on, and stare it down so that God's light and life would have the last word in Jesus's life, and through him for all of creation.

Finally, Jesus knew the importance of *prayer*, not as an external practice but as an encounter of the Father's love. No matter how great the crowds, the demands on his time and compassion, he knew it was essential to regularly withdraw from all other demands to pray. For all Christians, but especially for ordained leaders, prayer is pivotal to our faith, where Christ goes from an idea to a person we encounter in faith. It is from this wellspring of daily communication mediated by one's belief, time, space, language, and culture that those in holy orders deepen the primary relationship with the One whom they serve and so become more like Christ. It is in the intimacy of prayer that the ordained are invited again and again by God to cooperate with grace—for we are never coerced by it—and to see that, like Jesus, the depth of prayer will be demonstrated in how we live, the extent of our love, and our thirst for justice. As St. Francis of Assisi is reputed to have said, "Preach always and everywhere and if you must, use words."

Development of Ordained Ministry

Volumes have been written on how ordained ministry has developed over the centuries. For our purposes, there are three major moments, or developments, that saw dramatic innovation to the development of church structures and offices from the earliest to our present understanding of *church* and the wider world.

The first major development occurred when Jesus did not return as quickly as was expected. As the earliest Christians started dying, they had to attend to maintaining the authentic Christian movement by handing on the story and teachings of Jesus and establishing a pattern of leadership with authority to make decisions and maintain unity. They returned to the models they knew and still had before them: the temple priesthood of Judaism. In the Letter to the Hebrews, most possibly written just before the destruction of the temple of Jerusalem in AD 70, we have an excellent example of an early theologian reading back onto Jesus ideas about the ways the Jewish priesthood operated and how Jesus was the definitive high priest: "Jesus' death, the letter argues, was the sacrifice to end all sacrifices, revealing him to be at once priest, altar and sacrifice. The shape of church ministry was transformed by this theological development."[2] We find in the later New Testament writings a much more structured order of ministries, where the "royal priesthood" of all believers is administered by a cultic leadership where the sacrifice is now offered for the glory of God and the redemption of the world (see 1 Pet 2:5, 12).

The second major development of holy orders occurred in the second and third centuries where theological and political arguments raged and Christians were being martyred. Disunity could mean death, so a sometimes-underground church developed a more hierarchical structure. The most important officer to emerge was the *episkopos*, or bishop (the word in Greek means "supervisor"). St. Ignatius of Antioch outlines that these men oversaw the liturgical, moral, and theological life of all the house churches in a town or city. It is the women and men known as the deacons who were the bishop's most active assistants. Presbyters (priests) were not the usual presiders at the Eucharist but came to be so when the local churches grew to such an extent that the bishop could not be regularly present.

The third dramatic development occurred with our friend Emperor Constantine. As Christianity became the religion of the state, so too, as we have seen, the rights, responsibilities, trappings, and privileges of secular office crossed over to the church as well. Either by choice or direction, the church adopted much more clearly delineated roles for clergy and laity. Though ordination to holy orders is still seen to be intimately connected to the call and assent of the community, priests and bishops were also servants of the state, who invested them with juridical and administrative powers, so the local councils of presbyters, or elders, became secular leaders as much as they were ecclesiastical ones. The Council of Chalcedon in AD 451 was determined to maintain the most ancient link between the community and the call of its leaders. There is a wonderful legacy of that link in each of the three current rites of ordination. After a senior cleric declares to the bishop that the candidate has been tested and found worthy to be ordained, the bishop asks the assembly if they concur, and if so, they show this assent by acclamation. By ancient custom, if they withheld their applause, then the ordination did not proceed, or at least we know it was held up until the issues were resolved. Maybe contemporary communities should reclaim their voice and this ancient power. The patriarchal nature of Roman culture and its public leadership also has a strong impact on the demise of women's leadership in the church, especially as deacons, culminating in the Council of Laodicea (AD 352) where they legislate that women are not to be ordained.

Constantine wanted Christianity to unify his empire. The *episkopos*, or bishops, were often away from their fast-growing dioceses, attending local synods or ecumenical councils that set about settling theological and other issues that had beguiled Christianity for centuries. By the end of the fifth century, a unified church was a highly stratified institution within the Roman Empire and was as much about serving the state as it was serving Christ. The Order of Deacons was on the wane and the bishops and priests set about governing the church together. We had come a long way in five hundred years, and by this time, we reached the basic shape of holy orders that, with developments, still survives.

Ordination of Married Men

"In the Latin Church, the sacrament of Holy Orders for the presby-terate is normally conferred only on candidates who are ready to embrace celibacy freely and who publicly manifest their intention of staying celibate for the love of God's kingdom and the service of men." (*CCC* § 1599). While this statement is true of the current discipline in the Western or Catholic Church, it has certainly not always been the case.

While Jesus was celibate and acknowledged that some people might be so "for the sake of the kingdom of heaven" (Matt 19:12), we know by his practice that he did not insist on it. He called a married Peter. Mind you, I have always wondered about poor Peter's wife and children, if they had any. In leaving everything to follow Jesus, this seems to have included his spouse, which is not the family-friendly image the church promotes today. By tradition, we believe all the earliest disciples and apostles did the same.

Paul knows that mandatory celibacy is not required for being a leader in the Christian Church, but it is to be preferred for some. He states,

> I wish that all were as I myself am. But each has a particular gift from God, one having one kind and another a different kind. To the unmarried and the widows I say that it is well for them to remain unmarried as I am....
>
> But if you marry, you do not sin....Yet those who marry will experience distress in this life, and I would spare you that....
>
> I want you to be free from anxieties. The unmarried man is anxious about the affairs of the Lord, how to please the Lord; but the married man is anxious about the affairs of the world, how to please his wife, and his interests are divided. And the unmarried woman and the virgin are anxious about the affairs of the Lord, so that they may be holy in body and spirit....I say this for your own benefit, not to

put any restraint upon you, but to promote good order and unhindered devotion to the Lord ....

So then, he who marries his fiancee does well; and he who refrains from marriage will do better. (1 Cor 7:7–8, 28, 32–35, 38)

On one level, Paul's call to celibacy is utilitarian: the Lord will soon return, so while we wait and work there is little point to getting married and having a family. And even though Paul assumes that the leaders of the church are married men, and even uses their stewardship of their family as a metaphor of the leadership of the church, his closest followers, Titus and Timothy, were celibate like him for the sake of the mission (see 1 Tim 3 and Titus1:6–9). So, from the earliest days of the church, optional celibacy was the norm, where married and unmarried men, and we assume celibate and married women deacons, led the church.

It is not until the Councils of Elvira (AD 306) and Carthage (AD 309) that a law requiring celibacy for holy orders is enacted. Enforcing it was quite another matter. These laws were introduced because of the claims of deceased clerics' families on the property of the church. When a celibate cleric died, no such dispute arose, and so we can see why this latter option was judged best and necessary. It was also given a new theological reading that held that celibacy was a more radical following of Christ and enabled the cleric to have an undivided heart. However, these laws were met with resistance in many places and were not received easily, well, or at all. In AD 325, the Council of Nicaea decreed that after ordination a priest could not marry, and even by 385, Pope Siricius left his wife and children to become the pope. By the time of Pope St. Leo the Great (440–61), the law of celibacy seems to be the normative discipline in Rome. Even so, later decrees of the Council of Tours (567), Popes Pelagius (580), and the Synods of Metz (888), Mainz (889), and Rheims (909) addressed celibacy, married priests, and the wives and children of clerics. As late as 1045, Pope Boniface IX resigned in order to marry, and so dispensed himself from the requirement of celibacy.

The Eastern Catholic churches always remained more open to the ordination of married men and were suspicious of mandatory celibacy. In the fifth century, they begin the practice of only appointing celibates as bishops, who from the seventh century came from among the celibate monks. Though not universal among all Orthodox churches today, this process remains the norm, as it does for the Eastern Catholic churches who are in full communion with Rome: the Maronite, Coptic, Armenian, Chaldean, and Melkite Catholic churches. Though it is only a small part of the divisions between the East and West, the demand for universal, mandatory, clerical celibacy was one of many factors that led to the tragedy of the Great Schism in 1054.

While the Eastern church went its own way, the Western church, focused on reform, turned to enforcing celibacy. In 1020, Pope Benedict VIII reinforced the decree of Elvira, forbidding any inheritance rights for the children of clerics. However, in what must be one of the most tragic and evil of legal enforcements, Pope Urban II in 1095 had priests' wives sold into slavery and their children abandoned. Thankfully we know that many places and people disobeyed this immoral law. In 1123, the First Lateran Council decreed that all clerical marriages were invalid, and the final definitive law mandating clerical celibacy in the West, with the threat of excommunication, was handed down at the Second Lateran Council in 1139. By 1563, the Council of Trent taught definitively that celibacy and virginity were superior Christian states to marriage.

It has only been in the last hundred years that the Catholic Church has revisited celibacy and the teaching about sexual ethics and marriage that undergirds it. In 1930, Pius XI expressed the more ancient theology that sexual expression in marriage can be "good and holy" in itself. In 1962, John XXIII revised Trent's decree and declared that marriage was equal to virginity and both could be equal paths of great holiness. In 1967, Paul VI authorized the restoration of the permanent diaconate for married men in the Western church. In the 1980s, scores of married priests and ministers of other Christian denominations were ordained as Catholic priests and continue to live out their vocations to their wife and family as well as to their holy order. As our understanding of the origins and practices of the earliest church—of sexuality and of the Christian vocation—has developed, a reversion to the more ancient discipline of married and celibate clergy is to be preferred.

Ordination of Women

What follows is a brief and incomplete summary of the arguments surrounding the ordination of women to the priesthood.

There are six main reasons the church says it has no power to ordain women: first, Jesus did not ordain any women—that the first apostles were all male; second, the all-male priesthood has been an unbroken tradition in the church's history; third, because in sacramental liturgies the priest acts in the name and person of Jesus—having a male priest establishes a clearer iconography or identification between the priest and Jesus; fourth, while women and men are created equal by God, they have differing gender-specific roles, and to confuse these is to harm the balance of our human condition; fifth, the priesthood should not be seen as an office of power to be obtained and used, but as an order of self-sacrificing service; finally, the church has been a place where women are not oppressed but where their many and manifest gifts have flourished and been celebrated from Mary, the Mother of God, who is first among (all) the saints, to St. Mary Magdalene, who was the "Apostle to the Apostles" to an array of mystics, saints, founders, martyrs, and scholars.

The critics of these arguments claim, first, that Jesus may have had twelve male apostles, but he had and commissioned many female disciples, some of whom were his most faithful followers. They also challenge the claim that he "ordained" anyone in the way the church now uses that term and understands that office. Set against the customs of his day, his attitudes and practices toward women and their leadership were radical. Second, the argument of an unbroken tradition of an "all-male" liturgical leadership is not as watertight as some claim. There seems to be evidence of women presiding over house churches, Mary Magdalene and Junia are called apostles, and women were deacons for several centuries. Third, at sacramental liturgies, the priest acts in the name and person of the Risen Christ in whom "there is no longer Jew or Greek, there is no longer slave or free, there is no longer male and female; for all of you are one in Christ Jesus" (Gal 3:28).

Fourth, the church has let go of Jesus's culture and religion as prerequisites for Christian ordination, yet gender apparently remains the only nonnegotiable. Fifth, given that we no longer read the Book of Genesis literally, the gender roles that emerge there should not be absolutized, but should rather be interpreted as a theological construction around social determinations. Sixth, there is nothing wrong in talking about access to governance when it combines the right and just use of power as well as modeling self-sacrificing service. Finally, for all the church's rhetoric about the great gifts of women, and especially about motherhood, there has not been a corresponding and meaningful harnessing of their gifts for leadership at every level of the church's life. In a related argument, the theologian Elizabeth Johnson argues that the church cannot consistently make Christ's power to save dependent on some aspect of the humanity he assumed. If Christ did not assume attributes of humanity (even if, as a particular human, he could only embody some) then "whatever has not been assumed is not saved" and women (as well as others) remain outside the tent of salvation.[3]

In speaking with young people, both within and outside of the church, it is rare that this issue does not emerge strongly for many of them as a problem in their life of faith. They see that in nearly every other sphere of life women are, at least theoretically, now enshrined by law in most countries, and able to hold any office of principal authority in any institution other than religious ones. Certainly, some women and men have walked away from a faith in a so-called male God and some from the Catholic Church because they see it as inherently discriminatory.

Though the status of women is vastly different throughout the world, and sometimes criminal and tragic in some cultures, even within these differing social expectations, St. Pope John Paul II said that women's rights to dignity and human flourishing are given by God and should always be defended by the church.[4] This is even more true in nations where women's basic human rights are criminally and tragically abused. Given the differing social expectations, and even though the issues are larger than ordination, current debates, both inside and outside the church, often center on the church stating that it cannot—has no authority to—ordain women to the priesthood.

While the judgment of a male cleric might be seen to be overly defensive of the church's position, I want to revisit the earlier distinction between ordination and leadership. When I recall the greatest women in the Christian story who inspire me: Joan of Arc, Teresa of Avila, Catherine of Siena, Catherine McAuley, Mary MacKillop, Mary Ward, Nano Nagle, and Mary Aitkenhead, just to name a few, none of them were ordained and they all had to put up with appalling discrimination from male church officials of their day. The only historical comfort we can draw from what they suffered is that their detractors are now forgotten to history, but each of them is now or is in the process of being declared a saint, and rightly so.

Pope Francis has initiated a discussion on the role of women in the life of the church. "Women must have a greater presence in the decision-making areas of the church … [they] cannot be limited to the fact of being an altar server or the president of Caritas, the catechist.… No!…We need to create still broader opportunities for a more inclusive female presence in the Church….Demands that the legitimate rights of women be respected, based on the firm conviction that men and women are equal in dignity, present the Church with profound and challenging questions which cannot be lightly evaded" (*Evangelii Gaudium* 104).

In 1994, I was ahead of my time. After I had spoken at a conference entitled "Women and Men and the Future of the Church," I received a letter of sharp rebuke from the local bishop. I had argued that, given that the pope had recently ruled out the ordination of women to the priesthood, we should move apace to return women to the Order of Deacons and to readmit laypeople to the College of Cardinals—including, this time, laywomen. The bishop was incensed that I would present such "personal and maverick ideas" in his diocese. Within a few short years, I found myself in good company, with Cardinal Martini coming out in favor of women cardinals, and, more recently, in even better company, with Pope Francis opening the way to the possibility of women deacons. My ideas have turned out to be less personal and less maverick than the furious bishop thought.

Cardinal Martini and Bishop Emil Wcela have been voices calling for women to be readmitted to the ancient Order of Deacons for decades. "Ordaining women as deacons who have the necessary personal, spiritual, intellectual and pastoral qualities would give their indispensable role in the life of the church a new degree of official recognition, both in their ministry and in their direct connection to their diocesan bishop for assignments and faculties. In addition to providing such women with the grace of the sacrament, ordination would enable them to exercise diaconal service in the teaching, sanctifying, and governing functions of the church; it would also make it possible for them to hold ecclesiastical offices now limited to those in sacred orders."[5]

Women becoming cardinals is also both theologically and theoretically possible.[6] Regardless of this discussion, it is incontestable that women should participate more in church decision-making: locally, nationally, and internationally. Rather than walk away from the church, young women will hopefully stay, name, and shame any discrimination they experience in God's name, enabling all of us to create a more inclusive and empowering church for them and their daughters and sons.

Clericalism

In marketing these days, buzz words and taglines are everything: short, immediate disclosures that peak interest or point to a larger message. Whether it's intentional or not, Pope Francis is a master of this communication. When people both inside and outside the church think about Francis, words like *mercy, joy, compassion, care for the environment, a church of the poor for the poor*, and possibly even *reform* immediately come to mind.

There is another buzzword that he mentions just as much as these others: *rigidity*. While calling everyone in the church to be faithful to the gospel and the best of our received Catholic tradition, the pope rails against those who interpret, teach, or apply that tradition "with hostile inflexibility." He has addressed this vice in no uncertain terms to religious, young Catholics, liturgists, canon lawyers, and ecumenists, but it is to those in the sacrament of holy orders that he has particularly been upfront with the challenge: stop being rigid. Pope Francis sees rigidity as a symptom of clericalism, which he has called a "cancer within the church."

Regarding clericalism, the pope writes,

> This approach not only nullifies the character of Christians, but also tends to diminish and undervalue the baptismal grace that the Holy Spirit has placed in the heart of our people. Clericalism leads to homologization of the laity; treating the laity as "representative" limits the diverse initiatives and efforts and, dare I say, the necessary boldness to enable the Good News of the Gospel to be brought to all areas of the social and above all political sphere. Clericalism, far from giving impetus to various contributions and proposals, gradually extinguishes the prophetic flame to which the entire Church is called to bear witness in the heart of her peoples. Clericalism forgets that the visibility and sacramentality of the Church belong to all the People of God (*Lumen Gentium*, nn. 9–14), not only to the few chosen and enlightened.[7]

Confronting the rigidity of clericalism means those in holy orders need to be detached from ideology. I know clerics on the liberal and traditional extremes of our Catholic community who are equally rigid and clerical. For example, I know priests who cannot wear clerical dress under any circumstances and others who cannot but wear it. In their lives' context, custom and appropriateness count for nothing. They are equally unfree. Clericalism is where those in holy orders "'feel they are superior, they are far from the people,' they have no time to hear the poor, the suffering, prisoners, the sick. 'The evil of clericalism is a very ugly thing!…Today, too, Jesus says to all of us, and even to those who are seduced by clericalism: The sinners and the prostitutes will go before you into the Kingdom of Heaven.'"[8]

Almost every time Pope Francis raises the "cancer of clericalism," he usually also mentions a lack of freedom. This holds the Ignatian key to the very traditional and Catholic point he is making. The founder of the Jesuits, St. Ignatius Loyola, was given to scruples. At one stage, they were so bad that he was emotionally crippled by them. He wrestled against them for the last thirty-four years of his life, and he came to see that one of the great consolations of the Holy Spirit was freedom from rigidity, of being able to "let go and let God." With God's grace, Ignatius could appropriately deal with his ego insofar as he could rejoice at being a creature and not seek to act as the Creator. He knew interior freedom was one of the manifest signs of the Spirit.

Ignatius was convinced that attachment to earthly pride and ego, and in this case clericalism, saw those ordained into holy orders not being faithful, hopeful, and loving in our leading in Christ. Francis rails against young and old clerics in the church with little or no pastoral flexibility, because he believes it's a symptom of a spiritual disease that leads to being defensive and hypocritical.

> We must remember…that as clergy we all began our lives as lay people and that 'we'd do well to recall that the Church is not an elite of priests, of consecrated people, of bishops but all of us make up the faithful and Holy People of God'…. Clericalism [is] 'one of the greatest distortions affecting the Church…[because] it forgets that the visibility and the sacramentality of the Church belong to all the people of God and not just to an illuminated and elected few'….'It is not

the job of the pastor to tell the lay people what they must do and say'…'they know more and better than us'….'We are called to serve them [lay people], not to make use of them.'"[9]

Cinematic Clergy

Rather than take one film, I want to look at the bank of images built up over the best part of a century regarding the portrayal of clergy in the cinema.

Spencer Tracy was the first talking priest in the cinema. He was turning boys lives around as the heroic priest in *Boys Town* (1938) and *Men of Boys Town* (1941). Pat O'Brien tried to enlist street kids to become altar boys through the beauty of the Tridentine liturgy in *Angels with Dirty Faces* (1938). Bing Crosby went to the altar on the big screen twice in two years: *Going My Way* (1944) showed how music at the liturgy and the founding of a choir could convert young hoodlums and save a parish; and in *The Bells of St. Mary's* (1945), the attraction between (Sr.) Ingrid Bergman and (Fr.) Bing Crosby was handled in the most pastoral of ways. Rossellini's *Rome, Open City* (1945) has the clergy as leaders of the Italian resistance and the confessional as a way for secrets to be passed during the Nazi occupation. Gregory Peck, in *The Keys of the Kingdom* (1944), taught his congregation in China that Catholicism may be an ancient and European religion, but it can sustain you even to martyrdom. John Ford's controversial film *The Fugitive* (1947) centered on Henry Fonda standing up to a military junta and making a pastoral choice to baptize a woman's illegitimate child. Robert Bresson's *Diary of a Country Priest* (1950) showed the desolate Claude Laydu worn down by his obligations to the church and his parish. In *On the Waterfront* (1954), the director Elia Kazan presents Mass as a private devotion that sustained Karl Malden in tackling organized crime. *The End of the Affair*, Graeme Green's conversion story, has had two major movie makeovers—1955 and 1999—where the clergy help the hero discern his best choice.

As with the world in general, the portrayal of the clergy changed significantly from the 1960s onward. Igmar Bergman's *Winter Light* (1962) was a masterful but bleak picture of a Lutheran priest who mechanically celebrates sacraments that fail to give him comfort or hope as he loses his faith. A more upbeat priestly portrait comes in 1968 with *The Shoes of the Fisherman*, an adaptation of Morris West's novel of the same name. After decades in prison, Archbishop Kirill Lakota is released from a Siberian Gulag in time to be made a cardinal and attend the conclave in Rome where, as a compromise candidate, he becomes the pope. After the election of the Polish St. Pope John Paul II in 1978, this film was considered prophetic.

By 1973, Fr. Lankester Merrin and Fr. Damien Karras, in *The Exorcist*, must confront their personal demons as well as the devil to become sacrificial victims in setting twelve-year-old Regan MacNeil free of evil possession. This film spawned an entire genre. *Monsignor* (1982) shows a good man who loses his way morally and personally as he climbs the leadership ladder at the Vatican and ends up in bed with the mafia and a young nun. The following year, *The Scarlet and the Black* told the true story of Monsignor Hugh O'Flaherty, a priest who smuggled out thousands of Jews and Allied POWs through the Vatican during the Second World War.

The eighties and nineties gave us, by turns, clergy who were quaint, courageous, and criminal. Fr. Tim Farley, in *Mass Appeal* (1984), movingly has stopped being a "song & dance" priest so that he can love his people enough to tell them the truth. *The Name of the Rose* (1986) uses a fourteenth-century Benedictine monastery to explore not only a murder mystery but questions of the interplay between sex and death, unseen and unknown forces, and the role of humor in our lives. Fr. Adelfio, in *Cinema Paradiso* (1989), is the village pope and the local censor. The biopic *Romero* (1989) shows the courage of a saint and the price he paid for speaking truth to power. Archbishop Gilday flirts with evil in the Corleone family in *The Godfather: Part III* (1990). By 1991, it was time for the pope and the cardinals to be lambasted as goons for the mafia in the comedy road film *The Pope Must Die*.

Antonia Bird's *Priest* (1994) was a game changer where loneliness, child sexual abuse, the seal of confession, the crisis in celibacy, alcoholism, and despotic bishops and priests living double lives are forensically detailed. The Irish clergy are morally uncompromising in *A Love Divided* (1999), but *Molokai: The Story of Father Damien* (1999), starring David Wenham, is the true story of a pastor who not only became his people's advocate but also became their "fellow leper." In *Chocolat* (2000), Pere Henri is eventually liberated by a chocolatier who helps him find his own voice.

Keeping the Faith (2000) uses a three-way romantic comedy to explore issues of celibacy, interreligious dialogue, and a gentle exploration of the demands of ministry. *Italian for Beginners* (2002) might focus on a married Lutheran pastor, but it sensitively presents issues of evangelization, aging clergy, and being a priest who engages with the wider community, with all the challenges that can entail.

As the 2000s roll on, a fraudulent clergy is portrayed: *The Crime of Father Amaro* (2002), a priest who is tough on everyone else seduces a teenager and then arranges for an abortion. *Mystic River* (2003) was the first film to unmask an abuse ring between Boston's police and its clergy. *The Da Vinci Code* (2006) throws the book at the clergy for covering up everything all the way back to Jesus and Mary Magdalene, and Silas, the sharpshooting Opus Dei monk, has miraculous sight for an albino. Fr. Janovich has a lot to learn about pastoral tact in *Gran Torino* (2008).

Doubt (2008) is the film adaption of the 2004 play that explores child sexual abuse and what justice and knowledge demands of those who know the truth and those who think they do. Fr. James Lavelle, in *Calvary* (2014), has the most dysfunctional parish ever portrayed on the silver screen, within which he has to deal with a victim of sexual abuse who thinks he should die for the crime of another priest. While *Spotlight* (2015) is primarily about *The Boston Globe*, their real-life investigation of clergy sexual abuse is as searing as it is necessary. It won the 2016 Oscar for Best Film.

The last three films just discussed are but only an example of the predominant way Catholic clergy or church personnel have been presented as child abusers. Other documentary films include the following: *Twist of Faith* (2004); *Deliver Us from Evil* (2006); *Hand of God* (2006); *Sex Crimes of the Vatican* (2006); and *Mea Maxima Culpa: Silence in the House of God* (2013). Catholic brothers have also been similarly portrayed as physically violent or sexual predators in *Devil's Playground* (1976); *Heaven Help Us* (1985); *The Boys of St. Vincent* (1992); and *Song for a Raggy Boy* (2003).

Finally, when Fr. Montgomery tries to shame Mildred Hayes to take down her signs in *Three Billboards Outside Ebbing, Missouri* (2017), he has met his match, and maybe Mildred speaks for a generation whose trust we have lost:

> Y'know what I was thinking about today? I was thinking 'bout those street gangs they had down in Los Angeles, those Crips and those Bloods?...If I remember rightly, the gist of what those new laws were saying was...unbeknownst to you, one of your fellow Crips, or your fellow Bloods, shoot up a place, or stab a guy, well then, even though you didn't know nothing about it,...you're still culpable. You're still culpable, by the very act of joining those Crips, or those Bloods, in the first place. Which got me thinking, Father, that whole type of situation is kinda like your Church boys, ain't it? You've got your colors, you've got your clubhouse, you're, for want of a better word, a gang....And I don't care if you never did shit or you never saw shit or you never heard shit. You joined the gang. You're culpable. And when a person is culpable to altar-boy-fucking...then they kinda forfeit the right to come into my house and say anything about me, or my life, or my daughter, or my billboards. So, why don't you just finish your tea there, Father, and get the fuck outta my kitchen."

This incomplete survey tells a tragic story that needs to be told. It also demonstrates how the cinema is a social barometer, mirroring major shifts and issues for us. From heroic figures fighting social justice to idealistic pastors empowering their flocks, the cinema moved to looking at the changing nature of priesthood and celibacy and its costs, then to confronting evil without, and now to exploring evil within.

Conclusion

Men who receive the sacrament of holy orders are meant to be *alter Christus*, like Christ, in being: sacrificially loving in their service; obediently listening to God and the world; living the good news in a simple and direct way; empowering others, especially those who may be sinners—the least—or those who live on the margins of our church and society; confronting evil by advocating for a faith that does justice especially for the poor; and being prayerful, not through an external show, but of the intimacy borne of loving encounters with the Trinity. This call is an enormous challenge, a profound honor, and a sacred trust. Sometimes it can be overwhelming.

In fulfilling these calls, sometimes we hear those in holy orders—bishops, priests, and deacons—say, "I didn't want to be ordained but God called me and that was that." In saying this, I am not sure they have thought through the implications of this statement. First, God's call to any vocation never obliterates his great gift to humanity: free will. The call to ordination may be seductive, powerful, or terrifying, but we are always free to say no. God has other options; he wants us, he does not need us. Second, anyone who gets ordained to holy orders states they are doing so knowingly and freely. If any man feels coerced into ordination by God, family members, a community, or even the pope, then his ordination is invalid. So, it follows that, at some fundamental level, we need to want to be leaders in the Catholic community as deacons, priests, or bishops, and we need to purify our desires for why we want what we want. We do this by divesting ourselves of seeking prestige, honor, and power to imitating the radical servant leadership of Christ, standing with the poor and the oppressed, and empowering others.

Making sure that those in holy orders do not obscure the primacy of the baptismal priesthood of all believers, the sacrament of holy orders is at its best when it does not dominate the lay faithful but empowers them to be the church in the social, public, cultural, and political worlds. And as Pope Francis has said, for that we constantly need to generate "new forms of organization and of celebration of the faith."[10]

6

Marriage

BEFORE I BECAME a priest, I used to sing at weddings, and sometimes I was asked to sing some very strange things. The seventies and eighties were heady days! In the early eighties, many brides asked for Mary Magdalene's big hit from *Jesus Christ Superstar*: "I Don't Know How to Love Him," to which I would say, "If you don't, you shouldn't be here." Yet, consider the rest of the chorus: "And I've had so many men before." Too much information! "In very many ways." Oh please, this is getting worse. "He's just one more." I don't think this is what we really want to say at the sacrament of matrimony.

I was also asked to sing, "We've Only Just Begun" by the Carpenters, though I think this sacrament is more "than a kiss for luck and we're on our way." Then there was "That's Amore" by Dean Martin: "When the moon hits your eye like a big pizza pie, that's amore," or "Love Will Tear Us Apart" by Joy Division, and finally, the showstopping recessional, "Another One Bites the Dust" by Queen.

It was in 1981 that I was asked to sing the funniest song ever for a wedding. The bride requested the 1975 Donna Summer hit, "Love to Love You Baby." She gave me the tape, which was the media of the day, and I realized the words were not going to be hard to learn since they were an ongoing repetition of the song's title. That's it! That's the entire song until we get to the third verse, when Donna seems to have an ecstasy or orgasm. I knew about Teresa of Avila having ecstasies in her prayers, but she was a saint, and I was not, and this was at church on

Saturday. So I called the bride and said that "Love to Love You Baby" is not against faith and morals, but I am worried about the third verse. I then asked, "On Saturday, are you expecting me to do the ecstasy or not? To which she said matter-of-factly, 'Do you think you can?'"

These days the reality in the Western world is that there is no other sacrament where one often has to walk the line between the secular and sacred more than marriage. We may do baptisms and funerals for the people who have little or no contact with the church, but for the most part, they are happy to go with the ritual of the church when baptizing their child and their grief often moderates excessive demands at funerals, but more on that in the last chapter.

At marriages, the meeting of the wider world and the divine space happens long before the ceremony. In fact, it can be easily argued that, maybe including baptism, marriage is our most Evangelical sacrament, given that in most Western countries, the vast majority of couples and their guests do not come near a church, synagogue, or temple to get married these days, but 72 percent of all couples profess their public vows before an authorized civil marriage celebrant in a secular setting. So, even with mixed and complex motivations, it is generally a very good move of the couple to seek Christ's blessing of their marriage because we believe it is Christ who has initiated this movement to grace and Christ who is the actor at this and every sacrament. Mind you, some priests overstep their authority and act as though they "own" the sacraments. We are ministers of what Christ is doing here, and within the boundaries of what we can possibly do and for the good order of the sacraments, we should be as generous to those who do not tick every religious box in the same way that Christ called, healed, and included the same groups in his day.

I am often the second priest the couple sees. On finding out the couple are already living together, which is around 80 percent of most couples these days, the first priest tells them, "Well, we can't do your wedding in the Catholic Church until you stop living together, having sex, and you make a very good confession." Sometimes those couples walk out of that parish office right into the arms of the civil marriage celebrant. And sometimes they are referred on to me. While it would be preferable for the couple to take the priest's advice, I cannot understand why some priests are so demanding and unwelcoming, because even in terms of classical theology and canon law, here is a couple trying to regularize their relationship that the church considers to be irregular. I try to deal compassionately with them, encourage them to do the right thing by the church, but get them up the aisle.

Almost every couple who comes to see me tells me they want to do their wedding in a very "authentic" way. This usually means they don't read anything from the Bible and they want to sing "Kumbaya." However, I take them at their word and suggest we avoid all those wedding rituals that, these days, are totally inauthentic. I suggest that we not give away the bride. "Why?" asks a shocked bride-to-be. I always need to give them the history. "Well," I say, "that comes from when you were one of your father's possessions and he 'gave you away' to another patriarch for a dowry, often two pigs and a cow." Now I don't see any livestock trucks outside weddings anymore. Quite rightly, we are not bartering our daughters anymore because we own no one. But on the wedding day, a woman who may be wonderfully articulate about her independent feminist rights enacts one of the oldest continuous patriarchal rituals still operating in society. I can't even get most brides to get their mother and father to walk with them down the aisle. And I wish I could report that this ritual is now about the closeness of father and daughter, but that's not what I see at the rehearsal and at the back door of the church. I have had brides who have had to find their father first to come and give them away. Given the only person coming to the wedding who doesn't know that the bride and groom have been living a common-law marriage for the last four years is granny (and by the time it is all explained to her, the couple will be civilly and sacramentally married), I suggest that twenty minutes before the ceremony begins, the three of us gather at the back door of the church, welcome the guests, and distribute the orders of service. Then, once the processional hymn begins, the three of us process up the aisle, moving the couple from common-law marriage into civil and sacramental marriage. Even though this is totally authentic, wedding lifestyle wins the day, and so only fifteen couples have done it this way in twenty-six years. I lost that one.

Then comes the subject of the wedding rehearsal, where I suggest that we have it on the Friday night before the wedding. The groom gets in on the action: "Sorry Father, I don't think we can do that, because it's bad luck for me to see the bride within the twenty-four-hour period." "Give me a break," I say, "you've seen more of this bride than I care to know about." And then I tell him the history: "This so-called lucky day before the ceremony comes from when you never saw the bride. This was an arranged marriage and the first time you laid eyes on each other was at the lucky dip of the lifting of the veil. And by then it was too late because you had just been declared as husband and wife." He is having a heart attack at the potential bad luck he will have, so we're back on Thursday for the rehearsal.

On the wedding day, in walks the virgin queen, head-to-toe in white, wearing a veil over her face. I love it when most my brides wear veils over their faces because, when she gets to the top of the aisle, I want to explain the history of the veil. I tell the congregation, "We have all noticed that our bride is wearing a veil over her face. That represents her hymen, and he who at this ceremony will raise the veil will later break the hymen." In fact, I don't say that at the wedding! Even I have my limits, but I want to say it because it is such a good example of how, these days, the wedding lifestyle wins out over authenticity.

The final, sometimes uneasy, intersection between the wider world and the divine space concerns the cost of weddings. The average marriage across Western countries now costs $44,000. That's around $6,500 an hour, and the deacon, priest, or bishop is not the one bumping up the price. I have stood between two floral arrangements that cost more than I do. I readily concede I am not as beautiful as the flowers, but I speak. We now have families who are mortgaging their houses to pay for their children to get married. The most expensive place for a wedding is Manhattan, and the least expensive, in the Organisation for Economic Co-operation and Development (OCED), is in South Africa. While I am delighted that people celebrate this day well with their families and friends, I am anxious that the wedding industry exploits a misplaced belief that the amount of money a family has is comparable to the amount of love available or that the politics of envy see our expectations for the day outstrip what is just and right. So many weddings now seem to be royal weddings. And it worries me that some churches and ministers are also cashing in with exorbitant charges to "hire" the church or the minister. While I think a modest donation to the church for its upkeep is well within expectations, using any place of worship or sacrament as a moneymaking business for a parish undermines the nature of a place of worship and the integrity of the sacrament, all of which, officially, are meant to be free. Ministers who will not do a marriage or any other sacrament *unless* their fee is paid are guilty of the serious ecclesiastical crime of simony, and the punishment for that crime is dismissal from office. The couple and the church need to be on guard that the allure of riches does not blind them to the incalculable love we are celebrating in Christian marriage, and so resist the wedding industry as much as possible.

The Backstory

Marriage has quite a history, and despite what some Christians say, it has changed considerably over time. The Greeks were the first to reflect systematically on the affectionate bonds between human beings. They used seven different words to give meaning to the experience of personal attraction and emotional bonding:

> *eros* was sexual desire and passion;
>
> *ludus* was playful love where we enjoy each other or flirt;
>
> *philia* was the deep affection between committed friends;
>
> *agape* was sacrificial love, where someone was prepared to give something, maybe everything for another;
>
> *pragma* was a love that endures over a lifetime;
>
> *storge* was a protective and providing love like that between parents and their children; and

philautia was self-love, which was positive or negative depending on how one lives it.

Unfortunately, in English we increasingly just use one word, *love*, to describe all these various categories, feelings, attachments, and levels of commitment. We can see how some of these various categories apply to marriage, but not as neatly as we may think.

Some people argue that the institution of marriage provides the bedrock for society in the Old Testament. Jonathan Sacks, the chief rabbi in the United Kingdom, disagrees. He argues that the family was the bedrock of Hebrew society and that, in the Old Testament, there were a variety of ways to attain a family and a few models on what constituted a family.[1] God may have decreed in Genesis 2:24 that a man and a woman leave their parents and join themselves to each other and "become one flesh," but soon after other arrangements emerged. Abraham fathered children with his concubine as well as his wife. Moses had two and maybe three wives, but it is not clear if he had them simultaneously. However, the great patriarchs of Israel are not on their own. Abdon, Abijah, Ahab, Ahasuerus, Ashur, Belshazzar, Ben-hadad, Caleb, David, Eliphaz, Elkanah, Esau, Ezra, and Gideon, just to name a few, had multiple wives, lovers, and children, but Solomon seems to be the greatest of the polygamists having, it is claimed, seven hundred partners (1 Kgs 11:1–3).

As any polygamous world indicates, women in the Old Testament were possessions of their patriarch, who could marry them off for family alliances, political ends, and money. Women, at least not of royal blood, had no freedom to choose their husband or end a marriage.

As the Old Testament writing matures and Israel's society matures, marriage develops. Judaism moves from marriage being a political or familial contract to a reflection of the covenant God has entered into with his chosen people. Rabbi Sacks concludes, "Ultimately Judaism saw marriage as the supreme example of a covenant, namely a commitment based not on mutual benefit but on mutual belonging, whose key value is fidelity, holding fast to one another especially during difficult times because you are part of who I am."[2]

For the writers of the New Testament, marriage as a covenant is the immediate antecedent. Here, while monogamy was the goal, divorce is permitted and widely enacted, and sadly, women still had no rights to choose a husband or divorce him. Marriage as covenant also became the bedrock of the church's language regarding the emerging sacrament of marriage. John Donahue observes, "All the sacraments are covenants, in which the initiative comes from God and the commitments are to be lived out by those who 'affirm' or receive the sacraments. Marriage is perhaps the best human analogue to biblical covenants. People who have experienced already the gift of mutual love give to each other their whole selves, as Jesus gave his body and blood for those he loved."[3]

By the end of the Old Testament period, the norm had become that a betrothal occurred, for a man between seventeen and nineteen to a girl between twelve and fourteen. Women had no rights at all. Once agreed between the families, betrothal was legally binding. No religious ceremony within which the couple marry occurred, but once the dowry was paid, a wedding feast was celebrated and the marriage was consummated. In ancient Israel, everything was done in obedience to the Lord, but marriage never entailed rituals before a rabbi in the synagogue.

Surprisingly, Jesus has very little to say about marriage in the New Testament, and when he does, he simply restates the teaching from the Book of Genesis. Mark provides the oldest teaching we have from Jesus on marriage:

> Some Pharisees came, and to test him they asked, "Is it lawful for a man to divorce his wife?" He answered them, "What did Moses command you?" They said, "Moses allowed a man to write a certificate of dismissal and to divorce her." But Jesus said to them, "Because of your hardness of heart he wrote this commandment for you. But from the beginning of creation, 'God made them male and female.' 'For this reason, a man shall leave his father and mother and be

joined to his wife, and the two shall become one flesh.' So they are no longer two, but one flesh. Therefore what God has joined together, let no one separate."

Then in the house the disciples asked him again about this matter. He said to them, "Whoever divorces his wife and marries another commits adultery against her; and if she divorces her husband and marries another, she commits adultery." (Mark 10:2–12)

Jesus's main concern, here, is how divorce places women in a very vulnerable position within society where they were almost always left to a life of insecurity and poverty. Later, Matthew and Luke add that a divorce could be allowed for *porneia*, a broad term meaning "sexual immorality." The only other major teaching from Jesus about marriage comes in Matthew's Gospel when, in the apocalyptic texts, Jesus says that, at the end of time, marriage will not be necessary because the world will be consummated with the reign of God (see Matt 22:30).

Traditionally, the church has argued that Jesus's attendance at the wedding at Cana instituted Christian marriage (see John 2:1–12). Raymond Brown disagrees and claims, "Neither the external nor the internal evidence for a symbolic reference to matrimony is strong. The wedding is only the backdrop and occasion for the story, and the joining of the man and woman does not have any direct role in the narrative."[4] Nonetheless, this first sign in John's Gospel that occurs during a wedding feast does reveal important things about the sacrament of marriage. On the most superficial reading, it seems that Mary likes a party. She is the one who asks for the miracle. John says, "Now standing there were six stone water jars for the Jewish rites of purification, each holding twenty or thirty gallons" (2:6), which amounts to a total of 120 to 180 gallons. Given today's bottles, that would be seventy-five dozen or nine hundred bottles of wine and "you have kept the good wine until now" (v. 10). This story richly uses three great symbols: Wine in the Old Testament is always a *sign of joy*. The wedding banquet is always a metaphor for *the marriage of heaven and earth*, which has now taken on a definitive form in Jesus, the Son of God. Why does Mary ask Jesus for the miracle? *To save the couple from shame.* Even now, to run out of wine at a wedding would be socially embarrassing. In the time of Jesus, it would have been a public humiliation. Wherever Christ is, there is no place for shame, only conversion, just as disciples have in seeing this sign.

While marriages are always about the love of the couple, in Christian theology, they also mirror the marriage of heaven and earth in Christ—where the highs and lows, tears and joys, anxieties and hopes we live, are always shared by Christ who goes before us, behind us, and alongside us as we live our commitments. Moreover, at its best, Christian marriage is meant to be joyful for the couple, for their family, and for the wider world, and where Christ is present, shame should be no more.

St. Paul often uses marriage as a theological metaphor, but, as we explored in the last chapter on holy orders, because he thought Christ would return soon, he thought it was better if men did not marry unless they had to. In 1 Corinthians 7, he makes provision for divorce under certain narrow circumstances, and he often tells husbands to be kind and good to their wives and families. By the end of the New Testament period, we may not hear anything about marriage in general, but when Jesus had not returned and family life needed to go on, the First Letter to Timothy teaches that, within an emerging leadership structure of the church, "a bishop must be above reproach, married only once, temperate, sensible, respectable, hospitable, an apt teacher….Let deacons be married only once, and let them manage their children and their households well" (1 Tim 3:2, 12). Titus states that a leader of the church must be "someone who is blameless, married only once, whose children are believers, not accused of debauchery and not rebellious" (Titus 1:6). We can confidently conclude that, if the leaders of the Christian community were being exhorted to live in this way, they were passing on the good news to their flocks as well.

Later Developments

Given that Jesus has little to say about marriage in the Gospels, and the New Testament writers develop how that institution should be lived for Christians, it is not surprising that there were fierce debates in the early church about the nature and meaning of marriage. In fact, for a millennium, it was debated whether it was a sacrament at all.

As far as we determine, the early church has no specific rite for marriage. The first detailed description of an actual Christian wedding ceremony is in the ninth century. However, this does not mean the church was uninvolved. Considering that most people had a formal ceremony, it was a civil action administered by the Roman State. As with every other sacrament we have explored, things change with Emperor Constantine and especially with his successors. We noted that, when Christianity became the Roman imperial religion, deacons, priests, and bishops became local clerks of the Roman State, and hence, the name clerics has stuck to this day. The Code of Justinian (AD 529–34) is the basis for many contemporary systems of civil law. It outlines the age and terms of marriage: women from twelve and men from puberty; that consent is necessary (of the woman's patriarch); and that a dowry is proper. Various intermarriages between classes and with women in prostitution were forbidden. It states that children are in "the power," or are the possessions, of their parents and that illegitimate children have no claim on the father's estate. From the previously generous provisions for divorce, the code restricts divorce and makes allowance for a mutual divorce, but only if both parties never remarry. There is no question that the man's interests and prerogatives remain paramount, though there are penalties for spousal abuse, and, on a few narrow grounds, a woman can divorce her husband. Only once in the Justinian Code is religion mentioned or mandated: Christians were not allowed to marry Jews, consequently they lived apart from each other throughout the empire. This clause would later be the basis of deadly misunderstandings. Marriage within the Christian empire was formally codified as a legal contract with obligations, rights, and penalties, and local clerics, including religious clerics, had to administer this code on behalf of the state.

By AD 400, there was a new law requiring all clerics to have their marriages blessed by a priest, but it was not mandated for others. After the fall of the Roman Empire and the emergence of the church as the major governing authority, especially in the West, bishops were required to decide on conflicts over who could marry and, in cases of divorce, property disputes. In the fifth and sixth centuries, we know that clergy performed blessing ceremonies at wedding feasts, but these appear to be restricted to the ruling classes.

In the seventh century, the Holy Roman Emperor Charlemagne— who divorced once, was widowed three times, and had several concubines—attempted to enforce a law requiring marriage to have the blessing of a priest. It was honored in the breach. At the same time, theologians were warming to marriage as an instrument of holiness. The Gregorian Sacramentary (the Hadrianum, ca. 790) prays, "It is truly just and right, proper and helpful for our salvation. You have joined the marriage pact with the sweet yoke of concord and the indissoluble bond of peace, so the chaste fruitfulness of holy spouses might be preserved for the adoption of children. For your providence, O Lord, and your grace arrange both of these: generation adds to the splendor of the world, regeneration leads to the increase of the church."

By the ninth century, there were renewed fights over the land claims of the wives and families of priests, some of whom were supposed to have been celibate. At the same time, the church was being sued by the disenfranchised, illegitimate heirs of wealthy believers who had left tracts of land to the church in their estates, sometimes as reparation for sin. However, it is the case of the Holy Roman Emperor Lothair II where the church seized its moment to assert its control over marriage.

If you thought Henry VIII was the first king to have marriage problems with the pope, think again. In 862, Lothair wanted to annul his marriage to Queen Theutberga and marry his lover, Waldrada. Theutberga was childless. Waldrada had already become the mother to several of Lothair's children. Lothair imprisoned his wife on the trumped-up charge of incest. Neighboring kings and the local Synod of Aachen approved Lothair's annulment until his queen escaped and applied directly to Pope Nicholas II. The pope referred the matter to his own tribunal, which consisted of the archbishops of Cologne and Trier, who were relatives of Queen Waldrada. On the tribunal's recommendation, the pope refused to recognize the local annulment and ordered Lothair "under pain of excommunication" to take Theutberga back. He did, but sometime later, and no doubt under extreme pressure, the queen agreed to the annulment. In 869, Lothair went to Rome to get the new pope, Adrian II, to give his imprimatur to the annulment. He did so, but Lothair died on his way home, leaving no legitimate heir to his kingdom. It was then divided among neighboring kings. Theutberga died in 875. What held for kings had to hold for his subjects, too, and so the church's power over divorce and against polygamy, concubines, and adultery was now entrenched.

By the late tenth century, marriages were almost uniformly blessed by local clergy, with or without a Mass to follow. Here, a curious custom developed, harkening back to the civil roots of wedding ceremonies. Couples often exchanged their vows at the door of the church, and only entered the building at the end of the civil ceremony for the blessing of their marriage or a nuptial Mass.

By the twelfth century, the argument that marriage should be made a sacrament had reached a crescendo. As Joseph Martos states, "Relatively early in the history of Christianity, marriage was regarded as a sacrament in the broad sense, but it was only in the twelfth century that it came to be regarded as a sacrament in the same sense as baptism and the other official sacraments. In fact, before the eleventh century there was no such thing as a Christian wedding ceremony in the Latin Church, and throughout the Middle Ages there was no single church ritual for solemnizing marriages between Christians."[5]

There is no doubt that the civil and contractual ideas of marriage contributed to it not being regarded as a sacrament, but so did the opinion of several church fathers and theologians, most of whom were celibate. First, over the centuries, theological arguments were that virginity was the holiest way of life in the church, and therefore marriage was a necessary state for those who could not take the higher path. Second, they wrestled with what sort of sacrament it was and who, precisely, was the minister of it. At best, they believed that marriage distracted believers from being solely devoted to Christ and preparing for heaven, and often cited the Book of Revelation to support their case:

> And they sing a new song before the throne and before the four living creatures and before the elders. No one could learn that song except the one hundred forty-four thousand who have been redeemed from the earth. It is these who have not defiled themselves with women, for they are virgins; these follow the Lamb wherever he goes. They have been redeemed from humankind as first fruits for God and the Lamb, and in their mouth no lie was found; they are blameless. (14:3–5)

Not every church father was negative about sexuality and marriage, notably Clement of Alexandria in his *Miscellanies* 2–3, Lactantius in the *Divine Institutes*, and Methodius of Olympus in *Symposium*, all of whom see marriage as a remedy for carnal pleasure, but also state that it can be a path to holiness. However, and tragically, the extreme enemies of the flesh held sway for centuries, and still capture the imagination of Catholics today with very negative attitudes to all things sexual, marriage included. Origen of Alexandria (not a saint), who castrated himself so that he would not have physical temptations, and St. Jerome, in his *Letter against Jovinian*, regard all sexual desire as the punishment for Adam and Eve's sin. Therefore, anything to do with sexual pleasure and procreation was suspect and could only be redeemed by baptism and, best of all, living a life of chastity. This tension was inherited by St. Augustine in the fifth century.

Before his conversion, Augustine had a concubine for fifteen years and fathered at least one child. In his *Confessions*, he tells us he had intense sexual desires and was given to every form of sexual pleasure. After his conversion, he became a very different man, and maybe in his case, he needed to change. In the process, and in concert with the sexual pre-occupation of many before him in Christian theology, he viewed the carnality of the body and its pleasures with deep suspicion. Augustine believed that virginity was superior to marriage, but in his *On the Good of Marriage*, he says that the union of a man and a woman is "the first natural bond of human society." He argues that the most important function, "the one worthy fruit" of sexual intercourse, is children. However, he goes on to maintain that fidelity, "a mutual service of sustaining one another's weaknesses," is also a demonstration of God's manifestation of presence, as is the companionship that the best marriages enjoy. Strikingly, he also argues that marriage is a *sacramentum*, not a sacrament, but nonetheless he believes it a sign of the spiritual marriage between Christ and the church mentioned in Ephesians 5. It's because Christ can never divorce the church that Augustine holds that the Christian marriage bond should never be broken in divorce, though if that does occur, he maintains that the divorced Christian should never remarry or have sex again. On sexuality, chastity, and marriage, Augustine's writing is a mixed blessing. As Elizabeth Clark concludes, his writing "became decisive for all later teaching in the Christian West on issues of marriage and sexuality."[6]

Consequently, marriage was finally declared a sacrament in 1184 at the Council of Verona. The proclamation builds on Augustine's ideas of the sacramentality of marriage but finally upgrades it to the seventh sacrament, which now mirrored the seven days of Creation. The ministers of marriage were the couple, the clergy were the witnesses, and consent and consummation—that is, the free giving of the mind and body—were now constitutive elements of the new sacrament. However, the fight was far from over. Pope Innocent III declared that anyone who did not hold this teaching was excommunicated and that's exactly what happened to the Cathars at the Fourth Lateran Council in 1215. In the thirteenth century, Pope Alexander IV enacted canons against arranged marriages and argued that marriage was a sacrament between two people who entered it freely and knowingly, making provision for women to have some, albeit limited, say about their husbands. In the sixteenth century, Luther and the Protestant reformers rejected all but two sacraments as valid (Baptism and Eucharist). They did this primarily because they could not find a satisfactory text to support the claim that Christ had instituted the sacrament of marriage. While they were happy to bless marriages and wanted to eradicate clandestine marriages, they thought that marriage belonged to the sphere of the state and that, in cases of adultery, remarriage after divorce was possible.

The Council of Trent was the church's response to the Reformation. In 1547, during the seventh session of the council, it defined that matrimony was "truly and properly one of the seven sacraments of the evangelical law, instituted by Christ the Lord," and that the church had the authority to establish impediments to marriage, to dispense from them, and therefore, regulate marriage. It rejected divorce because of adultery. The council reaffirmed the necessity of the freedom of each spouse and that their consent had to be exchanged before a cleric and two witnesses. This teaching on marriage was in force until recent decades.

Before we leave this summary of a very complicated history, it is important to note that against what some people say, Christian marriage has changed significantly over the centuries. From being the preserve of the civil sphere as a secular contract; to the church increasingly blessing marriages as a remedy to those who cannot live the higher calling of virginity; to the church needing to regularize marriage annulments, disputes, and claimants among its clergy and ruling families; to it being declared a full and true sacrament, "a sign of grace, instituted by Christ and entrusted to the Church, by which divine life is dispensed to us," and later still, that weddings must be performed in public by a priest and before two witnesses.

Furthermore, the right and prerogatives in marriage have changed dramatically, especially for women. It is only during the post-Enlightenment, in the late seventeenth and eighteenth centuries, that love and happiness were promoted as the reasons why husbands and wives got married, but it was only due to the Industrial Revolution, when the middle class started to become more economically independent, that these factors became a reality.

Until the nineteenth century, people did not get married to be happy, women had no say about the arrangements, and, except for royalty, they had no rights in a marriage. It was only in the 1970s that most countries began to change the law to accept that the rape of a wife by a husband was a crime. For twelve hundred years of Christian history, monogamy, for most classes, was not regarded highly, and women could be divorced easily.

Contemporary Marriage

The marriage vows are stunning in what they ask:

I promise to be true to you,
in good times and in bad,
in sickness and in health,
for better or worse,
for richer or poorer.
I will love you and honor you
all the days of my life.

The problem with the theology of marriage is that it has been, and sometime still is, formulated by celibate men, who, by definition, have had no experience of being married, and some of whom were at least suspicious of this institution if not openly hostile. Reacting against the passages about marriage in the *Catechism*, married moral theologian Lisa Sowle Cahill summarizes the problem: "A crying need is an honest investigation of the human reality of marriage, incorporating testimony from married persons themselves, across cultures. The capacity of a human relationship to function as a sign of a divine reality must necessarily build on the nature of the human signifier itself. To say in effect that the infinite faithfulness of God to the church needs a created representation, and that, since Christian marriage has been chosen as the sign, it must in every case manifest properties which quite exceed the human reality as widely experienced, is surely to put the cart before the horse. The bond between mother/parent and child almost seems a better natural sign of the unity and indissolubility of God's love for God's people, especially as it implies an appropriate hierarchy, rather than the submission of women to men as Christ's image, a conclusion too frequently drawn from Ephesians 5."[7]

It is a brave Catholic cleric, therefore, who tries to express a contemporary theology of marriage. Rather, the Catholic psychiatrist and theologian Jack Dominian, husband and father of four and founder of the Marriage Research Centre in 1971, argued that marital love begins with the ecstasy of falling in love, which gradually becomes loving in terms of being a sustaining, healing growth and enjoying sexual intercourse. Dominian was one of the first Catholic thinkers to celebrate sexuality in marriage. "Sexual intercourse is the channel which ultimately directs and summates all the elements of sustaining, healing and growth....Thus for me every act of sexual intercourse gives life and occasionally new life arises. In making love, couples enter the very essence of God's love...sexual intercourse goes on for decades after the menopause, sealing the creativity of the couple's life, expressed with a type of love which God opened in his initial love of creation and continues to maintain it."[8]

Finally, if all this still sounds lofty and idealistic, the Institute of Family Studies undertook a fascinating survey of couples who have been married between fifty and seventy years and who regard their marriages as "happy." The survey asked them to name the top three attributes that they believe have seen them happily married. From third to first, the list goes as follows: gratitude, forgiveness, and love.

Gratitude. Please and *thank you* may be the two fastest disappearing phrases from the English language. The following survey interview response is priceless:

> I can't think of a time in my 60-year marriage that my husband hasn't said please and thank you. I have never felt

taken for granted. From making a cup of tea to having a baby [I would like to note a bit of a difference in effort between those two!], he always sincerely says please and thank you. It was a good habit we all got into in our family, and I notice my children insist on it from their children too. It is not about courtesy, as good as that might be, it is about dignity and respect.

Forgiveness. In this regard, the outrageous motto of the 1970 hit film *Love Story* comes to mind: "Love means never having to say you're sorry." That might have been fine for Ryan and Ali, but it is not the gospel of Jesus Christ, and true forgiveness is a key to happiness. Have you noticed how many books, TV shows, films, and social media sites are about revenge and retribution? For happy couples and families, love means we can and want to say we are sorry, and that the other person in the family can, and wants, to forgive. One respondent said, "In our 50-year marriage and 49 years of family life, we could never pretend that forgiveness has been easy. It has never been a magic wand we've waved over deep hurts, some hurtful decisions and harsh words. Forgiveness does not deny reality, it deals with it. From small annoying things to a few big moments, genuine forgiveness has been essential for us facing a crisis and not getting trapped there. It has enabled us to learn, grow, and move on."

Love. No surprise that love tops the list. One of the problems, of course, is that we have devalued the word *love*. We say we love our car, our house, and ice cream. We even say we love our dog or our cat. But we cannot love possessions or pets in the same way we give and receive human love. Whom do we really love? If we want to answer that question, we must ask another: "For whom would we die?" In my experience, that usually shortens the "I love you" list considerably. Moreover, if our dog or cat is on that list, we need therapy immediately! However, what we are celebrating in the sacrament of marriage is the greatest expression of human love—sacrificial love, where the couple, following the example of Jesus, says, "I love you so much I am prepared to sacrifice something, maybe everything for you."

Based on my years as a deacon and priest, Christian marriages don't just happen—they're created, assisted, supported, challenged, and encouraged. Married couples need support to live a lifelong, faithful marriage. As one step in that direction, I always challenge wedding congregations to go home and circle our calendars on the first anniversary of the couple with the intention that the couple receive, one year on, as many cards, calls, text messages, and emails as they did on the wedding day. This is one small way to continue encouraging them in this lifelong adventure and to remind all of us that the sacrament of marriage is not just between the couple and in the family, but, along with all sacraments, it belongs to all of us.

Annulments

Even though the Catholic Church now clearly teaches that we are bound by the words of Jesus: "I say to you, whoever divorces his wife, except for unchastity, and marries another commits adultery" (Matt 19:9), we have seen how the church over the centuries became increasingly involved in the administration of civil marriages. It is worth noting that church thinking on divorce was not uniform. Both Sts. Basil of Caesarea and John Chrysostom permitted divorce in various circumstances. It may have been surprising to learn how often bishops and priests became involved in the settlement of divorces. For a church that famously does not recognize civil divorce, the distance from the state was not always so stark and strong. Even though St. Ignatius of Antioch, in his Letter to Polycarp in AD 110, argues that the bishop has a role approving marriages, we noted the dramatic shift in the church's power over marriage came in the case of Pope Nicholas and King Lothair. While it is hard to find many significant cases predating this monumental one, we can assume that, over time, the church was becoming the final arbiter of the validity of marriage, especially for the ruling classes. The church's power, asserted so forcefully in the ninth century, remained constant for centuries, including when Pope Alexander VI annulled Louis XII's marriage to Queen Joan in 1498 so he could marry Anne of Brittany. Famously, Henry VIII asked Pope Clement VII to do the same for him in 1527. However, this pope was effectively the Holy Roman Emperor Charles V's prisoner in the Vatican, and Charles was the nephew of Henry's wife, Queen Catherine of Aragon, so the pope refused the request. The six-hundred-year nexus between the church's final authority over marriage was broken, and much more besides. In February 1531, Henry VIII proclaimed himself "Sole Protector and Supreme Head of the Church of England," and on May 23, 1533, Archbishop Thomas Cranmer declared that Henry VIII's marriage to Catherine of Aragon had been annulled.

As other Christian denominations recognized civil divorce or established their own processes for remarriage, the Catholic Church took a harder line on the indissolubility of the sacrament of marriage. However, because every sacrament can be declared null and void under strict conditions of intention, form, and matter, then so could marriages, but annulments became increasingly rare. Catholic jurisprudence amassed multiple norms and disputations about historical and other cases that may justify an annulment almost exclusively for the Catholic royal households of Europe.

By the nineteenth century, adultery was common, and a civil divorce and remarriage was often seen as scandalous. For centuries, the very few annulment cases that proceeded were determined by the Vatican's supreme court: The Sacred Roman Rota. In 1902, Pope Leo XIII summed up the previous four hundred years by declaring that "the marriage of Christians when fully accomplished...cannot be dissolved for any reason other than the death of either spouse" (*Dum Multa* 2, December 1902). While the 1917 *Code of Canon Law* takes considerable care concerning marriage, it does not relax, promote, or permit annulment for the wider congregation and clearly argues the primary purpose of marriage is procreation.

In 1959, St. Pope John XXIII not only called for the Second Vatican Council (1962–65), but also for a revision of the 1917 *Code of*

Canon Law. At the Council, the bishops debated the nature and intentions of marriage, the dramatic rise and increasing ease in obtaining civil divorce in the developed world, and the issue of divorced Catholics remarrying outside the church. The Constitution on the Church in the Modern World returned to marriage as first and foremost a covenant between God and the couple as well as between the partners. It recognized that there were complex mental health and other disorders that placed the bonds of marriage under great strain. They also taught that the first good of the sacrament of marriage was the love and good of the spouses and then procreation, going as far as stating, "Authentic married love is caught up into divine love and is governed and enriched by Christ's redeeming power and the saving activity of the church" (*Gaudium et Spes* 48).

In 1968, the Vatican offered the world's bishops a renewed system of regional tribunals, most of which would be charged with regularizing the growing number of Catholic requests for annulments. By 1971, matrimonial tribunals were operative in the United States, Australia, England, Canada, and France. In 1983, John XXIII's call for the review of the 1917 *Code of Canon Law* was completed. It contains 111 canons on marriage, more than any other sacrament. It codified the covenant theology of marriage from Vatican II—that marriage is a loving partnership for life and that couples need to be aware of their rights and obligations—and it streamlined the process for annulments.

On August 15, 2015, acting as the supreme legislator for the Catholic Church, Pope Francis simplified the annulment process even further and called on bishops to be as compassionate as the law allowed. In summary, he legislated that if both former spouses wanted the annulment to proceed, and the case was clear, the process should be resolved in a "briefer process" to be held personally by the bishop with streamlined procedures. He also required all processes to be provided free of charge, insofar as possible, and eliminated the need for an automatic appeal.

A Case Study: Miriam and Clarke

For some Catholics, annulments are not the stuff of dry, historical development and legalistic debates. They are matters about flesh and blood, real emotions and lives. During World War II, my aunt Miriam was one of hundreds of Australian women who fell in love with an American soldier. She married her Episcopalian (Anglican) army major at the side altar of the cathedral in 1945. He was dashing and handsome, and by the time it came for him to return to the United States in 1946, they were expecting their first child.

Upon arrival at her new home, Miriam found that her brave soldier was not as fearless as she thought. He was completely dominated by his aristocratic, Episcopalian mother who made it clear from the beginning that she opposed their marriage. Miriam's life in that family home was a nightmare. The tensions boiled over when Andrew was born. Regardless of the promises his father had made in Australia to have their children baptized Catholics, the soldier waged no war against his mother who declared that if any grandchild of hers was baptized a "papist," she would disinherit the three of them. The major surrendered to his mother and demanded that Andrew not be baptized a Catholic.

Miriam was devastated. She gathered together her few possessions, had her son hastily baptized a Catholic, and fled back to Australia. In 1950, by now a divorcée, she met Clarke, a wonderful man who wanted to marry her and be a father to Andrew. When they went to see the local monsignor, he told them they could not be married in the church, and if they contracted a civil marriage, they would be excommunicated. These were tough days—Catholicism was one of the reasons Miriam left the United States. In turn, the very church she had defended now shut her out. From 1951 until 1993, Aunty Miriam and her second husband did not receive any of the sacraments. After attending Mass each week for the first twenty-three years of their marriage, but not receiving holy communion, they just stopped practicing their faith. Who could blame them?

After I started studying canon law in 1989, I encouraged Miriam to instigate annulment proceedings. She did so in 1990. In 1993, her annulment from her army major was granted. A month later, Miriam and Clarke were finally married in the Catholic Church at a nuptial Mass. The small congregation knew that this couple had been away from the church for far too long, but we also knew that God had never moved away from them. At that nuptial Mass, Uncle Clarke's best man was my cousin, Andrew, who had been born in the United States in 1946. My uncle had legally adopted Andrew the day after he civilly married Miriam in 1950.

When the moment came for Clarke and Miriam to receive holy communion for the first time in forty-three years, all of us had tears streaming down our faces. We all understood that sacraments are not primarily about observing laws and regulations, but they're given to human, frail, and open hearts as signs of God's love and compassion.

Annulment versus Divorce

Because my aunty was married and had a child, there are some Catholics who wrongly argue that she had no case for an annulment. However, this declaration by the church that the sacrament of marriage was invalid is not a "Catholic divorce." Divorce says the once valid civil marriage contract is now dissolved. Annulment says that, though the marriage looked like a Christian marriage in form, and even length, from the start it did not have one or several of the essential characteristics for a sacramental marriage. A couple can be married for years, have ten children, and still rightly obtain an annulment. A civil divorce rips up the civil contract; the parties were married and now they are not. An annulment says that there were factors, often unknown to the couple on the day, which meant that they never had a full and true *Christian* marriage in the first place—the sacrament is therefore null and void.

Annulment is not a statement the couple makes about their marriage. After hearing the evidence, the church effectively says, "If we knew everything we now know about this marriage, the sacrament should never have been attempted." Though there are many obscure reasons for an annulment, the most common grounds these days are the following:

Lack of freedom

Lack of consent, where the couple were not saying yes to the same Christian concept of marriage

Grave lack of knowledge

Grave lack of psychological maturity

Lack of marriage consummation

If a marriage has never been consummated, then the couple can apply to the pope directly, not for an annulment, but for what is technically called a dissolution of the sacrament. It doesn't matter if the couple had sexual intercourse before they married, it matters if they have sex afterward. I like the fact that we have a sacrament where sexual intercourse is the final constitutive action of the rite: no sex, no marriage.

Furthermore, annulment says nothing about the legitimacy of the children from the marriage. For the church, children are gifts from God whether they are born into a married relationship or not. They can never be "illegitimate" in the eyes of God and the church. That is why we baptize any child presented regardless of the circumstances of his or her birth, or that of the parents. Legitimacy is an issue for the state, so the church annulling a marriage says nothing about the civil rights and privileges of a child born into a marriage. If the marriage was civilly valid when the children were born and registered, then the state recognizes them as heirs and successors. Of course, even legitimacy does not mean anything anymore because children born out of wedlock can make a claim on an estate, and, rightly, the courts often find in their favor.

If the couple do not fulfill the criteria of Pope Francis's reforms, some Catholics, and certainly most people who are not Catholic, cannot face the long, complex, and legal process involved in an annulment.

It can be a traumatic experience. Whatever of the process, as Pope Francis has repeatedly said, Christian teaching on this issue and its application to often brokenhearted people must always be metered with mercy and compassion. Personally, I think the church should step away from the legalism of witnesses, evidence, judges, appeals, and tribunals, which owes more to the Roman Empire than to the forgiveness of Jesus Christ. In its place, we might recognize how destructive behavior always contributes to the breakdown of marriages and so use the sacrament of penance and the ancient order of penitents to nullify the marriages that the church should never have celebrated, and that the couples sincerely know were never true sacraments.

Same-Sex Marriage

It is hard to think of an issue that presently divides the Catholic community more than same-sex marriage. In every state or nation where the legislature has debated or enacted same-sex marriage laws, the Catholic community has always been divided on the issue, sometimes in scandalous ways with brutal character assassinations and wild and bitter assaults on those who are perceived to be the enemies of the truth. Applying Christ's truth to contemporary issues of social policy and law should never see inexcusably ugly and uncharitable behavior. As St. Paul reminds us about all Christian disagreements, when we speak the truth, we are obliged to speak it in love, in charity (see Eph 4:15).

We have already established that the claims that "marriage has never changed" or that "Christian marriage has never changed" do not stand up to any level of historical analysis. Even when the church became involved in the administration of civil marriage and began to bless some marriages, they were also tolerant of certain classes taking other partners and royal men having concubines. It took centuries for Christian monogamy to become the norm for princes, and what was then good for them was good for their subjects.

There are a few scholars who argue that over time the church has blessed same-sex relationships. The late John Boswell of Yale University was the first major scholar to systematically study this question. In his *Christianity, Social Tolerance, and Homosexuality* (1980), *Rediscovering Gay History: Archetypes of Gay Love in Christian History* (1982), and *Same-Sex Unions in Premodern Europe* (1994), he cites more than sixty texts, the earliest dating back to the eighth century, that outline Christian commitment ceremonies that he argues were essentially blessing rituals for "same-sex unions." His critics claim that his desire to see these ceremonies as akin to modern-day same-sex marriages distorts his reading of the materials. Peter Steinfels writes, "There is no question that Professor Boswell has found records of ceremonies consecrating a pairing of men, ceremonies often marked by similar prayers and, over time, by standardized symbolic gestures: the clasping of right hands, the binding of hands with a stole, kisses, receiving holy communion, a feast following the ceremony. Some of these ritual actions also marked heterosexual marriages, but there remained differences in both actions and words between the two ceremonies."[9]

The reality is that these ceremonies, while fascinating in themselves, do not necessarily lead to the conclusion that they were same-sex unions or marriages. They can just as easily be read as commitment ceremonies for brotherhoods and fraternal associations, the existence of which, and the seriousness of the commitment therein, is also well documented over the same periods. We need to accept that these rituals were what they claimed to be—initiation rituals of a "spiritual or adoptive brotherhood."

There are a small number of texts denouncing homosexuality in the Old and New Testaments. However, further study of these texts suggests that what the author is condemning is pedophilia or rape. Even though the church now teaches that Catholics should treat gay people with "respect, compassion and sensitivity," there is also an irrefutable and shameful violent history toward homosexuals supported and promoted by the Catholic Church. Therefore, it is safer to conclude that until and unless we can prove that any fraternity blessing rituals led to homosexual couples living as spouses, then the tragic homophobia that has marked almost all of Christianity precludes seeing these liturgies as early Christian same-sex marriages. While marriage, both within and outside the church, has changed regarding its nature and form, rights and privileges, until the 1950s the "matter" for marriage has been consistently one man and one woman.

This leads us to contemporary, civil same-sex marriages. Given that the church's proprietary claims over marriage, which prevailed for eight hundred years, ended in the sixteenth century, and that since the Enlightenment of the seventeenth century religion is now but one of many claimants on the formation of social policy and law, we can see that, in a pluralistic, secular democracy, marriage has returned to the sphere of the state. This is largely consistent with the context within which early Christianity survived, prevailed, and thrived.

The Catholic Church has every right and obligation to hold and teach its developed doctrine regarding the sacrament of marriage: "The unique meaning of marriage as the union of one man and one woman is inscribed in our bodies as male and female.…The law has a duty to support every child's basic right to be raised, where possible, by his or her married mother and father in a stable home.…Jesus Christ, with great love, taught unambiguously that from the beginning marriage is the lifelong union of one man and one woman…[which indicates] the immutable nature of the human person and confirmed by divine revelation; hope that these truths will once again prevail in our society, not only by their logic, but by their great beauty and manifest service to the common good."[10]

I do not know a country that has mandated any religious organization to perform same-sex marriages or demanded that they amend their sincerely held religious views. The reality is that Catholics live in a society where many things that offend our religious convictions are now legal. Abortion, euthanasia, the mandatory detention and deportation of genuine refugees, adultery, capital punishment, premarital sex, divorce, nuclear proliferation, stem cell research, cloning, healthcare for all, and the care of God's creation for future generations are a few areas where the church's clear and strong teaching can clash with what civic law has approved, enacts, and enforces.

While we should always look to, argue, and defend the wider implications of every decision regarding the common good, the reality is that same-sex marriage is an action and decision within the domain of the secular state. What every developed nation says of marriage is an imitation of what we hold to be true about the sacrament of marriage. As far as I am aware, and though it may be assumed, there is no civic legal code of marriage anywhere that mentions the word *love* in describing this social institution. It would be hard for the state to legally mandate an emotion because if they did, and if that emotion were absent, the marriage would be invalid. First, the state must also make provision to marry people in arranged marriages, where the best hope is that love will develop later. Second, while much civil marriage legislation speaks of marriage as a "lifelong commitment," the state makes ample provision for quick and no-fault divorce. The lifelong character of civil marriage is at best a hope. Third, even before same-sex marriage, civil laws make no demand on couples being open to having children. Clearly, the state must marry couples who have no ability, intention, or desire to have children. Fourth, while marriage law often speaks about the couple "forsaking all others," adultery has been decriminalized in every OECD country except the United States, where it remains a criminal offense in twenty-one states, but where prosecutions are so extremely rare that the force of this law is nil. Finally, as unromantic as it may be, civil marriage law is contract law. If each party is of age, under no coercion, of full reason, and knowledgeable of the demand the civil commitment demands, they can sign the marriage contract. The couple are not actually married by the state when the celebrant says so, but when they sign the forms.

On the one hand, for that document to be legal, all that is required is some form of the vows made before an authorized notary or celebrant, and usually two witnesses of legal age. On the other hand, the church teaches that this sacrament is a covenant given by God and blessed by Christ for the spouses to minister to each other inasmuch as they are of legal age, have been prepared for the sacrament, are fully free, know to the degree that they are without reservations, are psychologically mature, and are open to children inasmuch as they can be. In such a case, they can enter into a lifelong and faithful heterosexual commitment. Civil marriage is *not* the same institution as the Catholic sacrament of marriage; not even close.

Celluloid Celebrations

There is no Catholic sacrament more than marriage that has been more influenced by the media's portrayal of it. It is not unknown for a priest to be taken by surprise when a bride preparing for marriage says her dress is being modeled on one in a recent movie or that of Kate Middleton's, and that the reception is going to be "under a marquee, like in *Four Weddings and a Funeral.*" The groom may say that he wants the music that was played at a wedding celebrated in a recent episode on television. There is, of course, nothing wrong with any of this, but by the end of the conversation it may be clear that the media is playing more than a consultative role in the decisions they are taking regarding the marriage celebrations. It can seem like the church is a set, the ritual is the script, and the priest is a supporting actor in a matrimonial matinee. Contemporary couples are not alone in being influenced by the media when they think of sacramental celebrations. However, cinematic portrayals of the sacrament of marriage are mixed blessings because the large or small screen directly shapes people's expectations of it.

When a church scene appears in a film, there is often no sense that the characters have any relationship with the presider or that they belong to the worshipping community that usually gathers in the church. There is often scant indication that the family or couple has any significant idea about why they have come to a church for a baptism or a wedding. Rarely do they demonstrate the Christian commitment they are celebrating in Christ's name.

Indeed, screenwriters and directors write and direct scenes for their characters using liturgical texts unknown to any mainstream

Christian church. They have incorrect vestments, know little about liturgical spaces, gestures, seasonal or ritual colors, and invent or minimize liturgical actions. It is possible to have an unrealistic expectation of television and film's interest in liturgy. These programs are not religious catechesis. Generally, they show liturgical actions as a way of situating characters as mainstream members of a community, or to open a plot line (a wedding or baptism), or to "kill off" a character (a funeral).

Arguably, the film that spent the longest amount of its time at church weddings was the British romantic comedy *Four Weddings and a Funeral* (1994). Here we are given a haughty Anglican bishop, Rowan Atkinson as a bumbling priest, the austerity of a Scots Presbyterian wedding service, a country wedding where the hippy singers belt out "Can't Smile without You," and a Christian funeral with a central and powerful eulogy. As enjoyable as this film was, apart from the clerical stereotypes, it stated that Christian liturgy is primarily about celebrating the lives of the couple or the memory of the individual. However, Christian liturgy, even at weddings and funerals, is always an action of the community of faith.

On one level, a film like *Four Weddings* underlines positively the need for ritual at important moments in people's lives. The use of Christian liturgy is due mainly to the audience's easy identification with the ritual and the opportunity to employ fine locations, sets, props, and costumes. The cinema faithfully shows the situation of a growing number of unchurched people who infrequently attend church. For them, the baby, the couple, or the deceased is the focus of the ritual. Consequently, many people these days cannot understand a minister's focus on the life, death, and resurrection of Jesus Christ, the believing community that gathers in his name, and the way in which these intersect with the liturgical action surrounding the baby, the couple, or the deceased. The cinema reinforces liturgy as one of many "social service centers" that people return to as needed. This is a serious and growing pastoral problem for the church.

Most seriously, the portrayal of sacraments on television and in film rarely gives any evidence that the liturgy changes people's lives.

Sacraments are reduced to social occasions and rites of passage, Christ is dislocated from being the center of the ritual action, the individual is worshipped, and their aspirations glorified. Anyone can join in because it makes no real difference to how we live away from the church. This undermines our belief that the sacraments "effect in us the change they signify."

Memorable religious weddings are featured in *The Philadelphia Story* (1940), *Father of the Bride* (1950), *West Side Story* (1961), *The Sound of Music* (1965), *The Godfather* (1972), *Steel Magnolias* (1989), *Father of the Bride* (1991), *Muriel's Wedding* (1994), *Emma* (1996), *Sense and Sensibility* (1996), *Love Actually* (2002), *My Big Fat Greek Wedding* (2002), *Les Miserables* (2012), and *The Big Wedding* (2013).

However, given that many of us think the cinema specializes in dysfunctional, abusive, and unhappy relationships, usually ending in divorce or death, there have been important explorations of faithful and long-lasting married love: *Guess Who's Coming to Dinner* (1967), *Fiddler on the Roof* (1971), *On Golden Pond* (1981), *Dying Young* (1991), *Shadowlands* (1993), *In America* (2002), *The Notebook* (2004), *Shall We Dance* (2004), and *Julie & Julia* (2009).

Surprisingly, one of the finest portrayals of the outcome of the sacrament of marriage is in the 2004 film *Hotel Rwanda*. Set in the genocide of almost a million Tutsis by machete-wielding Hutus in Rwanda in 1994, *Hotel Rwanda* focuses on, arguably, the only good news and true story to come of that evil horror. Paul Rusesabagina, the manager of a Belgian-owned Hôtel des Mille Collines in Kigali, is a Catholic Hutu. He is a dedicated family man married to his Catholic wife, a Tutsi, Tatiana. When the Rwandan president is assassinated, the country slides into chaos and racial violence.

Paul allows the hotel to become a haven for anyone he can save: Hutu, Tutsi, or foreigner. His wife and family are traumatized, and his house becomes crowded with Tutsi neighbors seeking refuge and leadership. He evacuates them all to the hotel where he tries to get his immediate family along with others safe passage out of the country via the United Nations. Tatiana will not leave Paul under any circumstances. When it becomes clear that the Hutu Paul could escape with his life, but that the Tutsi Tatiana would be killed by the mob, she says, "You could leave, Paul." "What are you saying, Tatsi?" "Your card says Hutu. Take our children, go and get the twins, pay money at the roadblocks. Get them out. Please." Paul replies, "Enough of this. We stay together. Let me rest, I will feel better then."

The final cards of the film read:

Paul Rusesabagina sheltered 1,268 Tutsi and Hutu refugees at the Hôtel des Mille Collines in Kigali.

Paul and Tatiana now live in Belgium with their children, Roger, Diane, Lys, Tresor, and their adopted nieces, Anais and Carine.

The genocide ended in July 1994, when the Tutsi rebels drove the Hutu army and the Interahamwe militia across the border into the Congo. They left behind almost a million corpses.

"You could leave, Paul."
"Enough of this. We stay together."
That's the power of the sacrament of marriage: love never ends.

7

Anointing of the Sick and Funerals

IN THIS LAST CHAPTER, we will combine the exploration of the funeral rites with the final of the seven sacraments, the anointing of the sick. We do this, first, not because I think they should be related, but because for many people, they are (more on that soon); and second, because, in a sense, death is the ultimate human healing. Celebrated within a requiem Mass or a Liturgy of the Word in the funeral service, it is arguably one of the most important moments for Catholics and potentially our greatest Evangelical outreach to those who usually never come near a church.

Strictly, the church has always understood the sacrament of the anointing of the sick as a continuation of Jesus's healing ministry. It was always meant to be about getting better. Maybe because later generations of Christians did not dramatically recover, as when Jesus and his disciples prayed over them, or our theology moved from a lively living of our faith in Christ to preoccupation on "saving our souls." In any case, by the twelfth century, this sacrament related to dying and the last chance for sins to be forgiven, hence it was called "extreme" or final "unction" or anointing. This emphasis was so prevalent in the Roman Catholic Church that we use to pray for what we called "the grace of a happy death." This meant a priest was in attendance to administer extreme unction, and provided our sorrow for our sins was sincere, we were told we would bypass purgatory or hell and go straight to heaven. In the medieval and Renaissance periods, there were royal and other wealthy families who had priests on hand whose most important task was to see that, no matter how terrible people had been in life, everyone received the "last rites" before death.

The exclusive connection between death and this sacrament continues today. I can go and see a friend or a parishioner in the hospital who is having serious but not life-threatening surgery. I offer to anoint them. Thinking I am suggesting they may die, they often say, "Unless they are not telling me the full story, I'm not that sick." Sometimes I can talk them around and we can celebrate Christ's healing gifts, but sometimes they sense receiving this sacrament is courting death and they do not want to tempt fate.

This unecumenical story humorously proves the point: Bubba was from Alabama. Although he was a good ol' southern Baptist, he loved the racetrack. One day while he was losing heavily at the track, he noticed a Catholic priest step out onto the track and bless the forehead of one of the horses lining up for the fourth race. Lo and behold, this long shot won the race. Bubba then noted the horse the priest blessed for the fifth race, placed some money, and won big time. As soon as the priest blessed the horse in the sixth race, Bubba raced for the window and laid down a serious bet. It won. Bubba was now in the zone. Before the last race he saw the priest step onto the track and bless the forehead, eyes, ears, and hooves of one of the horses. Bubba plunged everything he had won that day on that horse and couldn't believe it when the horse came in dead last. He was dumbfounded. He found the priest. "What happened, father? All day you blessed horses and they won. In the last race, you blessed a horse and he lost. Now I've lost everything, thanks to you!" The priest nodded wisely and said, "That's the problem with you Protestants, you can't tell the difference between a simple blessing and the giving of the last rites."

The idea of God coming to us in our suffering has long roots in the Old Testament. For prescientific religious people, everything they did not understand was given a theological reading ranging from floods, famines, and plagues to physical diseases and illnesses. God intended it to punish, warn, or teach his chosen people. The Book of Job is the best example of a theology that sees personal and physical suffering as God given. As poetic and moving as that work is, it is also a profound lament exploring heartbreaking theology.

The New Testament authors are in two minds about the sources of human suffering. In some instances, Jesus tells people not to sin again so that they will avoid future illnesses (see John 5:14); on other occasions, he rejects personal or family sinfulness as the cause for personal suffering. What we do know is that in every Gospel, Jesus is always moved to compassion by the person in front of him and tries to restore them physically, socially, and spiritually (see Mark 1:40–45; 9:14–29). Some miracles are associated with the person's great faith or the forgiveness of his sins (Matt 9:2–8). On other occasions, a healing is a sign of the kingdom of God (Matt 11:2–6).

The anointing of the sick is directly related to Jesus's healing ministry. It is clear from the Letter of James that this ministry was institutionalized and ritualized very early in the life of the Christian community: "Are any among you sick? They should call for the elders of the church and have them pray over them, anointing them with oil in the name of the Lord. The prayer of faith will save the sick, and the Lord will raise them up; and anyone who has committed sins will be forgiven" (Jas 5:14–15).

In his Letters to the Corinthians, St. Paul speaks about those who have a charismatic healing ministry. We have records from both Hippolytus and Tertullian in the late second century describing how prayers were said over the sick and they were anointed with oil. In the fourth century, arguably because people were not physically being healed as described in the gospel, John Chrysostom moved the emphasis of the sacrament from physical to spiritual healing. In the fifth century, possibly for similar reasons, the rituals and descriptions of the rite shifted again from the central element being the prayers over the person and the imposition of hands to administering the holy oil, "the medicine of the Church" as

Caesarius of Arles calls it. This sacramental oil begins to take on almost magical properties, often applied to the part of the body that was most diseased or in pain. An interesting fact that we know from Pope Innocent I's letter to Decentius, Bishop of Gubbio, is that while the bishop and the priests blessed the oil, laypeople could also administer this sacrament.[1]

As we noted earlier, in the fourth century, theology moved from the intimate image of Jesus as our servant and friend to seeing Christ as King, dispensing justice from the throne of grace within the heavenly court. Understandably, this developed after the baptism of Emperor Constantine and Christianity had become the imperial religion. Over the centuries, Christianity increasingly emphasized our unworthiness of Christ's presence and how he will judge all of creation. In the Carolingian period (ca. AD 780 to 900), people who were dying started to receive the sacrament of penance followed by the anointing of the sick. There appears to be no expectation that the ministers of the sacrament thought the sick would recover, so these rituals increasingly become preparatory rites before death. By the tenth century, only a priest could give the three sacraments to the dying: penance, anointing, and finally, holy communion. To this day these rites are movingly called the viaticum, or food for the (final) journey. Peter Lombard, in 1150, appears to be the first person to coin the phrase the "last rites" or "extreme unction," which became common. In the twelfth century, the rite makes no mention of any physical restitution and only speaks of spiritual healing, primarily through the forgiveness of sins. It is also during this time that holy oil is applied to each of the five senses including the hands and the feet because it was argued that all these were ways by which people commit sin.

In the sixteenth century, the Council of Trent restored to this sacrament an understanding of the physical healing proper to its history, allowing not only those who were in danger of death to be anointed but also those who had other illnesses. However, this wider permission did not flourish, and it remained the sacrament of the dying until the 1960s.

The Second Vatican Council commissioned a revision of every sacrament with a movement back to each of the sources. On November

30, 1972, a new rite was produced under the new name: the sacrament of the anointing of the sick. Pope Paul VI moved the focus of the sacrament away from the dying to the seriously ill and the elderly. Though the administration of the holy oil is the central ritual element within the rite, it is applied only to the hands and forehead, and now readings, prayers, and songs are suggested and encouraged. Communal rites of anointing were promoted and have become standard weekly features of many parishes. The 1983 *Code of Canon Law* understood this sacrament as one, albeit very important, element in our pastoral care of the sick.

In 1992, the *Catechism of the Catholic Church* insightfully saw the parallels between the sacraments of initiation into the life of the church and the sacraments given at the end of life. "Just as the sacraments of Baptism, Confirmation, and the Eucharist form a unity called 'the sacraments of Christian initiation,' so too it can be said that Penance, the Anointing of the Sick and the Eucharist as viaticum (Communion received at this moment of 'passing over' to the Father) constitute the end of Christian life 'the sacraments that prepare for our heavenly homeland' or the sacraments that complete the earthly pilgrimage (§1525). Later, the authors summarized a contemporary theology of the sacrament by stating that the special grace of the anointing of the sick is in how it links our human suffering to Jesus on Good Friday, who went through pain and death ahead of us. In it, Christ gives us strength, peace, and courage to carry the cross of illness, old age, or preparing for death. In this sacrament we are forgiven of anything that stops us from fully embracing Christ's life, and for the first time in centuries, we are encouraged to hope that we could be restored to health (§1532).

Kevin Irwin summarizes this theology:

> It is in the liturgy of the anointing of the sick that we learn what is of real value in life in the sense that those anointed become sacramental signs to the rest of the Church and to the world that productivity, prowess, and performance are of little value compared with identification with God in suffering, in allowing suffering to teach us reliance on God and

that the notion of 'human frailty' is really both redundant and eminently hope-filled. Those anointed remind us about who we really are—those who experience divine life here and now and who are destined for the fullness of this divine life in eternity with God forever.[2]

Expectant Faith and Miracles

One of the problems with the sacrament of the anointing of the sick is how it became disconnected from the actions of Jesus, who laid his hands on the sick, prayed for them, or just said they would be healed and it happened. Not that it happened every time. There are occasions when Jesus could not perform a miracle; so if miracles are simply a question of God's power, then we could always expect Jesus to be able to perform them. The gospel writers often put the lack of the miracle happening to a "lack of faith," which allows for other preconditions for a miracle to occur. However, Jesus generally heals those presented to him, and he certainly told his disciples to do so: "Then Jesus called the twelve together and gave them power and authority over all demons and to cure diseases, and he sent them out to proclaim the kingdom of God and to heal" (Luke 9:1–2). This is further developed in Matthew: "Jesus summoned his twelve disciples and gave them authority over unclean spirits, to cast them out, and to cure every disease and every sickness….'Cure the sick, raise the dead, cleanse the lepers, cast out demons'" (10:1, 8). And they went out and did just that.

The seventy disciples return saying they performed miracles (see Luke 10:17–20), and later we are told the twelve apostles healed the sick (see Mark 6:13, John 14:12) and that many signs were done by them (see Acts 4:30, 5:12–16). Peter and John heal a man who was crippled from birth (3:2–11). Peter heals the bedridden Aeneas (9:34) and brings Tabitha (Dorcas) back to life (9:36–42). Negatively, and unlike any event in Jesus's life, Peter strikes down Ananias and Sapphira for lying (5:1–10). Without details, we are told Stephen performed great signs and wonders (6:8). Philip cast out demons and healed many people (8:6–7, 13), and then he had a miraculous transportation (8:39). In Acts 19:11–12, we are told Paul healed many people including the father of Publius (28:8). Sadly, Paul strikes his enemy Bar-Jesus blind (13:6–11), but more positively heals a crippled man (14:8–10), casts out a demon from a female slave (16:18), and raises a young man to life (20:9–12).

Miraculous healings became much rarer as the Christian generations rolled on, and because of their paucity, the church had to rethink the expectations and reasons for this healing sacrament, even to the point of only reading it in spiritual and penitential terms. Problems always arise when our prayers are not answered, so we often say that we were asking for the wrong thing, that God said no, or he gave us what we really needed rather than what we wanted. It can also be said that we did not do enough prayer or the right type of prayer in the right way. We might think that we should have fasted more and undertaken more penance, and then God would have answered our prayer.

Our prayer is not about asking—or telling—God what to do and getting him to change his mind. The traditional Christian doctrine of immutability holds that God is, in essence, unchanging. This was a defining break with Greek and Roman theology and a development from the God in some parts of the Old Testament. God's unchanging nature is essential for the sake of our relationship with him and our sanity. This affects our prayer. I believe that all the sacrifices and prayers in the world cannot change God because that is the way God wants it. The Apostle James says, "Every generous act of giving, with every perfect gift, is from above, coming down from the Father of lights, with whom there is no variation or shadow due to change" (Jas 1:17). Our fasts, penances, sacrifices, and prayers are important, not because they change an unchanging God, but because they change us to be more open and receptive to God's love and life, which is constantly available.

Even though we have rightly reclaimed that physical healings can come through the anointing of the sick, we have limited expectations that it will actually happen. Our lack of expectation is a mistake. For me, this interest is not a fascinating abstraction; it is personal. Due to a car accident, my sister was left a quadriplegic for twenty-eight years. She died in March 2017. I prayed, fasted, begged, and wept for a miracle for her. Though she was one of the finest people I ever knew, a miracle never came her way.

One reason we have gone cool on expecting healings is because miracles raise issues about how much God intervenes in our lives and acts in a way that appears inconsistent with the laws of nature that, under God's care, have been set in place. They also challenge our concept of prayer, especially the efficacy of petitionary prayer, both here on earth and in heaven.

That miracles occur seems beyond dispute, especially in the realm of physical, emotional, or spiritual healing. In classic Christian dogma, the believer is required to affirm that miracles happen and that the author of the miracle is God. I can affirm both easily. I do not, however, believe that they come from without. I believe God works miracles from within. I have no concept of God "zapping" people with miraculous power. Such an idea can reduce God to a magician, gaining the admiration of the spellbound audience who longs to see his next amazing trick. One of the many problems with this model is that the most deserving people I know, like my sister, never seem to be called onto the celestial stage. I also reject this "magic model" because it cannot be found in the actions of Jesus. "Sign faith" in John's Gospel was considered the weakest faith of all.

Contemporary neuroscience is just starting to understand the general properties of the brain and this organ's potential to heal. Miracles occur when some of these healing assets are released by the brain into the body. For some, the reception of the sacrament of the anointing of the sick unlocks these properties. For others it may be a pilgrimage to a holy place, personal or intercessory prayer, devotion to a saint, or, for other more secular people I know who have experienced a miracle, it was a complete change in lifestyle, diet, and the practice of meditation.

This goes some way to explaining why Jesus could perform some miracles and not others, and why, at Bethsaida, Jesus had to heal the man born blind a second time. Even an encounter with Jesus or a single touch was not enough for some people, while for others their master's or friend's desires to see them well was enough to affect the change. Given that Christians readily concede that the evolution of the human brain is among God's greatest handiwork, then God is in every sense the author of the miraculous.

Of course we have enshrined our expectation of the miraculous in the process of making saints. For mystics and saints of heroic virtue (but not for martyrs), there is a requirement for a physical miracle. There are those who argue that the demand for a physical healing is too narrow. In Dublin, the intercession of the saintly Matt Talbot may not have produced too many cures from cancer, but there are hundreds of people who attest that through his intercession their loved ones have come to sobriety and stayed that way. Anyone who has lived with a chronic alcoholic can appreciate the miracle of such a transformation. Conversely, there are others who hold that if God is going to perform miracles through the intercession of prospective saints, we do not just need a cure here and there for a blessed few, we need more miracles for everyone. I have no problem believing that our companions in heaven, the saints, continue to pray that we might be open to God changing us so that, in the power of God's grace, we can change the world. It becomes a question of where God's grace resides. It is not just from without. Brian Doyle captures the same sense: "We think of grace arriving like an ambulance, a just-in-time delivery, an invisible divine cavalry cresting a hill of troubles, a bolt of jazz from the glittering horn of the creator, but maybe it lives in us and is activated by illness of the spirit. Maybe we're loaded with grace. Maybe we're stuffed with the stuff."[3]

The writers of the film *Bruce Almighty* were inspired when they placed these words on the lips of God: "Parting your soup is not a miracle, Bruce, it's a magic trick. A single mom who's working two jobs and still finds time to take her son to soccer practice, that's a miracle. A teenager who says no to drugs and yes to an education, that's a miracle. People want me to do everything for them. What they don't realize is *they* have the power. You want to see a miracle, son? Be the miracle."

SOS

Given our understanding of healing miracles in the broadest sense of being healed and how they may become manifest in our lives, I have no problem also believing that death is the final and greatest healing. Anthony Kain notes this connection: "In Christian healing, sickness loses its destructive power, its negative hold over us. Ministry to the sick seeks to transform the destructive symbol of illness into a life-growth symbol. The Sacrament of the Sick is an invitation to transformation, to conversion. And it is not even too much to hope that physical health can be restored even in the face of overwhelming odds....We remember, however, that in Christian healing, death is seen as the final healing."[4]

The problem has been that we have been too quick to turn this sacrament into our "ticket to heaven," or to pray for the "grace of a happy death" with a priest in attendance.

Not that I have any problem believing in heaven. If we can have one universe, it is plausible that other universes may exist. Even secular scientists are now positing (but have yet to prove) the existence of multiverses, and I believe that one of them is what we have traditionally called the afterlife. There is no question that the way in which the Christian afterlife has been presented by some Christians over the millennia was as a form of social control, but those days are now passed.

If there are some Catholics still preaching hellfire and damnation as the reason for faith, they must be disappointed that few people are listening to them. The rates of religious practice—often the way a believer tried to keep an angry God on his or her side and thereby avoid hell—have plummeted in almost every western country. Contemporary theology does not focus on being driven by fear but by being drawn by love. I am not a Christian simply because I am trying to "save my soul" from hell. My Christian belief is my response to a loving God's invitation to faith, hope, and love. Even when heaven, hell, and purgatory were presented graphically, there were problems with the literalness of the images. Classical theology has always held that eternal life does not consist of time and space, mind and body. Heaven is about transcending the bounds of earth. So even when preachers talked about "fire and brimstone" and "physical pangs," it was a poetic description of the indescribable because we cannot undergo physical torments if we don't have a physical body.

Our Catholic theology about heaven, hell, and purgatory enshrines a profound religious truth—that our life here on earth impacts our eternal life.

Certainly God would not deny heaven to the many people we know who lived their lives faithfully, lovingly, and hopefully as best as they could. The Scriptures give us confidence to know that God does not concern himself with small matters. But what about the individuals and societies whose behavior destroys other people? What about those who never repent of the sexual abuse of a child, their physical and emotional violence, or being a serial adulterer or murderer? What about those who refuse to share from their excess with those who have nothing in our world? And what about those who don't care or don't want to know about the fallout from their apathy or the consequences involved in the luxury of ignorance? None of these people, none of us, is ever too far from the compassion and forgiveness of God, but I am also convinced that God takes very seriously our free decisions on serious matters.

Before offering reflections on heaven, hell, and purgatory, let us consider the "soul." If eternal life transcends time and space, and mind and body, we cannot "do time" in purgatory and need to clarify what survives us when we die. Christians have always said that while our body dies, our spirit or soul survives and endures. In an increasingly secular society, two things are striking. The first is that for all the significant inroads aggressive atheists have made into religious and spiritual beliefs, young people, who may not express their spirituality within established religious collectives as in previous generations, have been flocking to the cinema for decades to see science fiction/fantasy movies. This genre is predicated on other worlds, other beings, this world and the next, metaphysics, metaethics, souls, spirits, angels, and other modes and forms of existence. The second striking reality is how the word *soul* persists in ordinary conversation. Many nonreligious people use this most religious of terms to describe another person. We often hear how others are lonely, distressed, or lost souls. It can be said that someone has a "beautiful soul" or that a piece of music, a painting, or other works of art "stirred my soul." We describe mellow jazz as "soulful" and still alert others to distress by an SOS, "save our souls." These uses of the word reinforce St. Thomas Aquinas's teaching that the soul makes us human and sets us apart from other animals. Nearly all the great religions of the world believe in a soul, or its equivalent—something that survives the annihilation of the body in death.

Whatever else might characterize the soul, memory is an integral part of it. Why? I have done several funerals of people who have suffered from Alzheimer's disease. These are rarely very sad occasions because the family invariably says that they "lost" their loved one months or years ago because, increasingly, their loved one couldn't remember anyone or anything. There are now theories about how even the memories of the circumstances of our conception and birth have a bearing on the way we live our lives. It is also apparent that, even when people seem to have lost their memory or are unconscious, there is recognition of some things at a deep level.

I readily concede that my position raises the question of the humanity of someone who cannot remember anything. Are they any less human? Every human being has inalienable rights because they may have memory at their deepest level and because we know in faith that each one is known and remembered by God from conception to death. So what happens after our soul leaves our body and is "commended to the mercy of God," as we used to say in the funeral rite? The great parable of God's mercy is the best starting point.

In the story of the prodigal son, we have the worst kid in town making a return and being received by his foolishly loving father. Rather than think of heaven, hell, and purgatory as places where we do time, imagine if they are experiences or states. I wonder if a goodly number of souls, people who have done their best on earth, make the journey home. The Father rushes out to greet them. They start their speech, but the loving Father cuts them off and welcomes them home. That must be the experience of heaven—welcomed to the eternal banquet!

However, some make the journey home and start the speech, which the loving Father allows them to finish—such has been the enormity of their deliberately chosen, free, and seriously destructive behavior toward others and themselves in this world. At the end of the speech they are forgiven, now fully aware of the gravity of their sinfulness and its impact. And it costs us to say, "I'm sorry," and it costs the Father to forgive—like a husband or wife who genuinely forgives the other for adultery. That might be purgatory—an experience in cleansing, of being purged, not in anger or suffering, but in love—painful love as it might be.

And for a very few who, throughout their lives have deliberately and knowingly rejected God—in all his forms: faith, hope, and love—make the journey to the Father and come face-to-face with pure love. They do not start the speech, they are not welcomed, because God respects their freedom so much that he allows them to do what they have done all their lives—see love and walk away. That must be hell—to know love, to have glimpsed it, and turn around and walk away because they always have. The ultimate absence: a remembering soul who saw love and chose otherwise.

I am in good company in believing that heaven, hell, and purgatory are not places we go to do time, but states we enter or a process through which we pass. Pope Benedict XVI agrees: "Eternity is not an unending succession of days in the calendar, but something more like the supreme moment of satisfaction, in which totality embraces us and we embrace totality...life in the full sense, a lunging ever anew into the vastness of being in which we are simply overwhelmed with joy" (*Spe Salvi* 12).

Memory as a constitutive part of our soul means that when I meet God face-to-face, I will remember who I am and how I have lived, and God will remember me. It's also a comfort for us to know that we will be reunited with those we have loved who have died before us, because we remember each other. Therefore, the experience of salvation is in part a purification of memories, where God "will wipe every tear from their eyes. Death will be no more; mourning and crying and pain will be no more, for the first things have passed away" (Rev 21:4).

God's Embrace

The first funeral I ever did took place a week after arriving as a deacon at St. Canice's parish in Kings Cross, the red-light district of Sydney. I was asked to do a "pauper's funeral," an appalling Dickensian name for a state-funded cremation.

Karl was an alcoholic and homeless man who had died on the street. The two saintly religious sisters who had cared for him for years organized his funeral.

The sisters thought it unlikely that anyone else would attend. On the day, there were three more mourners present. After the readings and prayers, and because I had never met Karl, I invited the congregation to share their memories of their deceased friend. Toward the back of the chapel the sisters shook their heads. It was too late. A short, stout woman was on her feet and was next to the coffin. "Thank you very much Father," she said deferentially, and then she let loose. "Karl," she yelled, pointing at the coffin, "you were a bastard. You were a bastard in the morning, a bastard in the evening, and a bastard at night time." And this theme, and that word, went on and on. The sisters started crying with laughter and gave me a look that said, "You got yourself into this; get yourself out of it."

After two minutes, I stood up and moved toward the eulogist, she took the cue and said, "So, in conclusion, I'd like to say, Karl, you were a spherical bastard, because anyway we looked at you, you were a bastard." And with that, turned to me and said sweetly, as though she had just delivered a loving tribute, "Thank you so much Father," and sat down. The sisters were in hysterics.

Esme had been Karl's wife. They had both been lawyers. I knew by her sophisticated use of the word *spherical*, that she was an educated woman, but they had both been codependent alcoholics and they blamed each other for the way their marriage and their adult lives fell apart.

This was quite a way to start my ministry to all souls. I wondered if all my funerals were going to be this action-packed. Luckily, since then, I have mainly buried spherical saints.

Talking of saints and sinners highlights the current understanding of funerals. The ritual hasn't changed, but our language has. Catholic funerals were occasions for praying for our deceased relatives and friends that they might not be in hell or have long in purgatory. Given the first option, there was not much any of us could do about it. Mind you, we have never had to believe that any human being is in hell. Most of our prayers at funerals asked that they soon be "released" from purgatory and admitted to heaven. This understanding changed after Vatican II. Where we once spoke of "commending our sister or brother to the mercy of God," or "praying for the departed's immortal soul," we now sound much more confident about where our sister or brother is.

I was struck by this theology during the homily delivered at Pope John Paul II's requiem Mass in St. Peter's Square on April 8, 2005, where some people were chanting *"santo subito,"* "sainthood now,"— indeed he was canonized, along with John XXIII, by Pope Francis on April 27, 2014—and the eminent theologian, Cardinal Joseph Ratzinger, who two weeks later became Pope Benedict XVI, said in his homily that Pope John Paul II was already enjoying heaven. "We can be sure that our beloved Pope is standing today at the window of the Father's house, that he sees us and blesses us." But that means he was already in heaven, which is what canonization says. I didn't disagree with him regarding Pope John Paul, but at no stage did he say that we "commended him to the mercy of God," or that we had to "pray for his immortal soul." Cardinal Ratzinger was perfectly in line with the recent change of emphasis at our funerals.

After Vatican II, we rediscovered a newfound confidence in God's compassion toward the dead. If we really believe in the power of Easter, then God's love at work in the world is greater than our sinfulness and our human limitations. As Christians, we know that love took human form in Jesus Christ. In other words, we have a God who not only entered our life but also was subjected to and embraced the alienation of death. We are the only world religion to believe this. Johannes Baptist Metz summarized this theology:

> Jesus did not cling to his divinity. He did not simply dip into our existence, wave the magic wand of divine life over us, and then hurriedly retreat to his eternal home. He did not leave us with a tattered dream, letting us brood over the mystery of our existence. Instead, Jesus subjected himself to our plight. He immersed himself in our misery and followed man's [sic] road to the end. He did not escape from the torment of our life, nobly repudiating man. With the full weight of his divinity he descended into the abyss of human existence, penetrating its darkest depths. He was not spared from the dark mystery of our poverty as human beings.[5]

Such was his commitment, Jesus did not simply and only come to die. Rather, Jesus came to live, and because of the courageous and radical way he lived his life and the saving love he embodied for all humanity, he threatened the political, social, and religious authorities of his day so much that they executed him. This is an easier way for us to make sense of the predictions of the passion. Jesus was not clairvoyant; he was a full and true human being and therefore had informed but limited knowledge. His full and true divinity cannot obliterate his humanity, or he would be playacting at being human. His divinity is seen in and through the uncompromisingly loving, just, and sacrificial way he lived within the bounds of his humanity.

When good people ask how a loving God could do such terrible things to them, some Christians will avoid the answer and simply tell them to "offer it up." Essentially, they are saying, "Well, God required Jesus to suffer a torturous death, so you must see in your own suffering and pain God offering you the same cup of suffering as he offered

Jesus." It is not that long ago that these ideas had such currency that we "offered up" our suffering for the salvation of souls in purgatory or for others whose lives we thought had offended God.

My concern, here, is not that Jesus suffered and died, and that so do we, but what sort of image of God emerges from understanding our salvation in terms of the commercial transaction of paying a ransom, or an angry God deriving satisfaction from us "offering up" our suffering, illness, and pain that he has sent to us in the first place. Another traditional way of understanding our suffering is to say that we are freely uniting our sufferings with the sufferings of Jesus so that they take on some meaning. If my thoughts on why Jesus suffered hold true, we could reclaim that style of approach but with a significant difference. Rather than the implied belief that our suffering is about the further appeasement of a needy God, which is difficult given that, classically, Jesus's sacrifice was once and for all, our suffering finds meaning by being faithful to Jesus's way, truth, and life, when every other instinct wants to cut and run. Here we find God in my Gethsemane, enabling me to confront death, destruction, and sin head-on, and holding to the experience of Jesus in that just as God had the last word of life in his dying, God will utter the same word about my dying too.

Once we replace the question "Why did Jesus die?" with "Why was Jesus killed?" the last days of Jesus's suffering and death take on an entirely new perspective. We can celebrate a funeral and listen to Jesus in John's Gospel say, "I have come that you may have life, and have it to the full" (see 10:10). This life is not about the perfect Son of the perfect Father making the perfect sacrifice to get us back in God's good books, thereby saving us. Our God does not engage in death, but in life. The New Testament demonstrates this, even the grand apocalyptic narratives about the end of time that possess the hallmarks of an inspired rabbinic teacher drawing big strokes on the largest of canvasses. Jesus did not intend us to take this imagery literally. Presumably, the experience of judgment will not actually be a livestock muster of sheep and goats. The lesson behind the imagery, however, is a real one for us to learn. God's compassion and love will ultimately see that justice is done.

He will hear the cry of the poor and we will be called to account in the next life for what we have done and what we have failed to do in this life.

At Catholic funerals, our hope is founded on how we find God in Jesus Christ confronting evil, death, and destruction head-on, staring it down so that God's light and life, which had the last word in Jesus's life, through him, will have the last word for us and all creation.

While Jesus was the most innocent of humans, we, through our destruction and sinfulness, most certainly are not. Nevertheless, when we come face-to-face with love itself, God will allow each of us to start the speech of contrition, as noted earlier. However, like the story of the prodigal son, some will not be allowed to finish our apology and be welcomed home; some may be allowed to finish; and a few may walk away from love because that's what we have always freely and knowingly done in life. Mercifully, none of us are obliged to believe that any human being is in hell. Therefore we are confident that God's full knowledge, compassionate justice, incalculable mercy, and complete love will have the final word.

All of this is easier to proclaim and celebrate when the funeral is that of an elderly person who died peacefully after a long and good life. It is severely challenged at the funeral of someone who has taken his or her life. The Catholic Church used to consider suicide as an act of despair and refused to bury the deceased from a church. Priests were only allowed to do prayers at the graveside. However, we now know that suicide is very rarely a deliberate, knowing, and free act, so the deceased and his or her family deserve from the church the compassion and love of God and all the support we can give them. Research we have from people who attempt suicide is that they did not want to die, they wanted the pain to stop. When they decided that the only way for the pain to cease was to die, they can be lost to free choice, to weighing up their options, and they become powerless to the force of their depression.

It is hardest to proclaim and celebrate when the funeral is that of a child, at any age. No parent should bury their child. For the record, God does not need angels in heaven. In theology, we say that God is sufficient. God does not need anything, and therefore, he has no need to take our children from us in any way, shape, or form, angelic or otherwise. What is exciting about Christian faith is that we believe God wants us. That is why humanity was created. Why would God's desire "to take" a two-year-old to heaven be more than God's desire "to leave" this child in the arms of loving parents? If God is into taking and calling the children we love in death, why not include those who are physically and sexually abused from the youngest ages by their evil parents and families, or who are orphans standing up in their cribs with outstretched arms and with no one to cuddle, love, or adopt them?

In contrast, it is entirely appropriate to believe that life, from the womb to the nursing home, is not allotted a span, as such, by God, but that our body will live until it can no longer function, for whatever natural or accidental reason. God is not an active player in this process, but, again, must take responsibility for making us mortal. In classical theology, the alternative would have been for us to have been created a disembodied spirit or an angel. But then I would not be me. Therefore I do not believe that God kills us off, but that, as painful as death is, we know that we will see our brother or sister again, and that Christian hope says that our parting is not a definitive "goodbye," but more a "see you later."

Until Death Do We Part

In films, it is not uncommon for a priest to be hovering around a bed giving the last rites. Not much is usually made of it besides a ritual background to alert the spectator that the end of the character is near. Only in a few films has the anointing before death been given attention: *Brideshead Revisited* (1981), where Charles Ryder says, "You said just now that the least shock would kill him. What could be worse for a man who fears death, as he does, than to have a priest brought to him—a priest he turned out when he had the strength?"; in *Shadowlands* (1993); *Dead Man Walking* (1995); *Marvin's Room* (1996); and *Camino* (2008). Consistent with development of this sacrament, there is not a film that I can recall where the anointing of the sick has been administered with the expectation or result that the sick person will recover. It is always presented as the ritual ticket to heaven. There are a host of films about the Evangelical preachers who claim to be healers, but they are almost always found to be frauds.

However, Christian, Catholic, and church funerals in movies generally tend to focus not so much on the ritual but on powerfully delivered eulogies.

The funeral in *Four Weddings and a Funeral* was held in a church for Gareth, who died of a heart attack while dancing at the wedding of Carrie to Sir Hamish Banks. His partner, Matthew, delivers a deeply moving eulogy, even more so because he did not write most of it. Like so many eulogists, Matthew turns to poetry to express his love and loss, reciting in its entirety, W. H. Auden's stunning, if bleak and hopeless, poem, "Funeral Blues":

> Stop all the clocks, cut off the telephone,
> Prevent the dog from barking with a juicy bone,
> Silence the pianos and with muffled drum
> Bring out the coffin, let the mourners come.

> Let aeroplanes circle moaning overhead
> Scribbling on the sky the message He is Dead,
> Put crêpe bows round the white necks of the public doves,
> Let the traffic policemen wear black cotton gloves.

> He was my North, my South, my East and West,
> My working week and my Sunday rest,
> My noon, my midnight, my talk, my song;
> I thought that love would last for ever: I was wrong.

> The stars are not wanted now; put out every one,
> Pack up the moon and dismantle the sun,
> Pour away the ocean and sweep up the wood;
> For nothing now can ever come to any good.

Maybe not surprisingly, two of the best films about the ritual of death and funerals come from Asia, where death has not been as privatized as in the West. In the Chinese film, *The Road Home* (1999), Luo Yusheng returns from Beijing to bury his father, Luo Changyu, who was the longtime teacher in the village. Yusheng's mother, Zhao Di, insists that her husband be buried in the village where they met. Luo Yusheng argues that the family is not wealthy enough to pay for pallbearers to carry a full day, trudging through the heavy snow. Zhao Di insists. Meanwhile, word goes out that the teacher's body is to be brought home. Former students volunteer their services for the procession. Despite a blinding snowstorm, everyone turns out. Moved by the veneration given to his father in death, Yushen fulfills his father's last wish: that the son become a teacher, if only for a day. He does so in the schoolroom where his father taught all his life.

The Road Home is not just a complete film about the rituals of death and farewell, it is a study on the fourth commandment: honor your father and your mother. Zhao Di knows the love her husband's students held for him, and so at his death, she gives them an opportunity to be generous.

While not explicitly religious, there are rich parallels between the village ritual and a requiem Mass: the coffin is bound in a special cloth, a pall. Symbols of the teacher's life are held and carried with each of them evoking stories that eulogize him. The central element of the funeral is the procession, where he is carried in love. And meals play a significant role in remembering Luo Changyu in the same way that the Eucharist of a requiem Mass nourishes the friends and family to continue to live lives worthy of the deceased.

The Japanese film *Departures* (2008) begins at the moment of death, with the slow, solemn, and deliberate ceremonial ritual of the Japanese undertaker. Daigo, a cello player, loses his job when his orchestra is disbanded. Unable to find any other work, he returns to his hometown and, through a mix-up, becomes an apprentice to Yuriko Uemura, the local *nōkanshi*, or traditional mortician.

He learns the ancient Buddhist art of the "coffinator," where the body is not just prepared physically, but where the corpse is prayed for, honored, and respected. Every religious action and meticulous movement of the *nōkanshi* is pregnant with symbolism and reverent assistance to the spirit of the dead as they move through the gateway of life to the next stage of his or her existence. As Daigo learns his craft of accompanying the dead, we find out about his life, from childhood illnesses to his tough upbringing by his father, his marriage, his family life, and even the music, which sees him come most alive. On learning that the father who abandoned him as a boy has died, he reconciles with him in death as he tenderly prepares his father's body for burial, embracing a healing and intimacy in death that escaped them in life.

The sweeping cinematography in both these films reminded me of the relationship between the honor Catholics pay to the body in our funeral rituals and its relationship to the created order from which it came: "earth to earth, ashes to ashes, dust to dust."

Is it any wonder that at the moment of farewell, Christians are often consoled by the ancient Celtic words that express this relationship and our hope that we will be caught up in it too:

> May the road rise up to meet you.
> May the wind be always at your back.
> May the sun shine warm upon your face.
> May the rains fall soft upon your fields,
>   and until we meet again,
> may God hold you in the hollow of His hand.[6]

Conclusion

LET'S CONCLUDE this book where we began—at baptism. I recently heard the story of parents who gave birth to a healthy baby boy. The father, Chris, was a very active member of his local Catholic school and parish in Fort McMurray, Alberta, Canada. Not long after the birth of their son, he and his wife, Christine, enrolled in the parish's baptismal preparation course and attended the first session. During the conversation that night, Chris heard that provided you have the right intention in performing a baptism—you preferably have a witness, use water, and invoke the Father, the Son, and the Holy Spirit—then any Christian can validly baptize another person.

Within a week of that baptismal preparation session, a wildfire began southwest of Fort McMurray on May 3, 2016. Initially, Chris and Christine thought their home was safe, but without warning, the winds suddenly and dramatically changed and their home was now in the direct line of fire. Chris tells the story that as he evacuated his wife and his son, he cradled his boy in his arms and whispered to him, "I don't know what's going to happen next, but I'm going to do everything I can to save you." As they rushed out of their home, Chris baptized Charlie. It took seconds to do. The world's newest Christian was already dealing with an unpredictably harsh world. This family successfully fled with their lives, which is ultimately all that matters. A father's promise to protect his firstborn child physically and spiritually meant they survived a baptism of fire.

This story of an emergency baptism is a perfect parable about what every sacrament does in our lives. They save us in every way from the power of evil, from our own destructiveness, from a life devoid of meaning and hope, and they prepare us for our Christian mission in a sometimes tough world, and ultimately for life with Christ for eternity. All seven sacraments either give birth to grace once and for all—baptism, confirmation, marriage, and holy orders—or can be received as often as necessary in living out our life in Christ—Eucharist, penance, anointing of the sick. In every encounter, we ask the Father, Son, and Spirit, who is unchanging in faithful love, to change us so that we will transform the world. Moreover, the church teaches that sacraments are foretastes of the heavenly liturgy (cf. *CCC* §1136) where we participate in a partial way that "your kingdom come, your will be done on earth, as it is in heaven." We hope and pray that every assembly that celebrates these sacraments rises to the invitation to mission as we stand in awe and wonder at the deep mystery of God, is as hospitable to others as God is to us, expresses an ancient faith that promotes faith and justice, and celebrates God's presence not just in heaven but also in our experience of real life.

Some people may think the title of this book on sacraments is flippant or glib. It is neither. What the ordaining bishop says to the candidate in the ordination rites is exactly the song we should sing at every sacrament: "May God who has begun this good work in you, bring it to completion." May that be true of us as these Christ events hatch us into new life, match our lives to be more like Christ's, and actively prepare us for the moment when we are dispatched into life eternal.

Notes

Introduction

1. Antonio Spadaro, SJ, "A Big Heart Open to God: An Interview with Pope Francis," *America*, September 30, 2013, https://www.americamagazine.org/faith/2013/09/30/big-heart-open-god-interview-pope-francis.

I. Baptism

1. Clare Watkins, *Living Baptism: Called Out of the Ordinary* (London: Darton, Longman & Todd, 2006), 28.
2. Sally Welch, *Every Place Is Holy Ground: Prayer Journeys through Familiar Places* (London: Canterbury Press, 2011), 10.
3. Sally Welch, *Every Place Is Holy Ground*, 9.

2. Eucharist

1. John Francis Collins, *Call and Response: An Introduction to the Catholic Faith* (Strathfield, Australia: St. Pauls Publications, 2010), 83.
2. Didier Rimaud, "In Remembrance of You," trans. and set to music by Christopher Willcock, SJ (Portland: OCP Publications, 1988).
3. Gerard M. Goldman, "Church: Seeking First the Kingdom of God," *Compass* 44, no. 2 (2010): 8.

4. Pedro Arrupe, SJ, Address to the Forty-First International Eucharistic Congress in Philadelphia, USA, in 1976.

5. Clifford Geertz, *The Interpretation of Cultures: Selected Essays* (New York: Basic Books, 1973), 114.

6. Frank Wallace, *Encounter, Not Performance: Frank Wallace SJ on Prayer* (Newtown, Australia: E.J. Dwyer, 1991).

3. Confirmation

1. Gerald O'Collins and Mario Farrugia, *Catholicism: The Story of Catholic Christianity* (Oxford: Oxford University Press, 2003), 140–41.

2. Patrick Fahey, *Rites to Life: Sacraments and Us* (Homebush, Australia: St. Pauls Publications, 1993), 31–33.

3. Anthony Kelly, "The Holy Spirit in Today's World," *The Summit* 37, no. 2 (May 2010): 3–4.

4. John W. Kiser, *The Monks of Tibhirine: Faith, Love, and Terror in Algeria* (New York: St. Martin's Press, 2002).

5. St. Benedict, *The Rule of St. Benedict*, Prologue 45, accessed August 9, 2018, http://www.abbaziamontecassino.org/abbey/index .php/en/worship/montecassino-blog-live/13-worship.

6. St. Benedict, *The Rule of St. Benedict*, Prologue 21, 49–50.

7. Kiser, *The Monks of Tibhirine*, 220.

4. Penance

1. Kenneth E. Bailey, *Poet and Peasant and through Peasant Eyes: A Literary Cultural Approach to the Parables in Luke* (Grand Rapids, MI: Eerdmans, 1983), 157.

2. Monika Hellwig, "Penance and Reconciliation," in *Commentary on the Catechism of the Catholic Church*, ed. Michael Walsh (Collegeville, MN: Liturgical Press, 1994), 274–87.

3. Peter Adam as quoted in Barney Zwartz, "The Resurrection of Sin," *The Age*, March 21, 2008, http://www.theage.com.au/articles/ 2008/03/20/1205602568458.html.

4. Adrian Lyons, *Imagine Believing: Explorations in Contemporary Faith* (Melbourne, Australia: David Lovell, 2003), 173–74.

5. Andre McGowan as quoted in Zwartz, "The Resurrection of Sin."

6. William Uren as quoted in Zwartz, "The Resurrection of Sin."

7. John Chrysostom, "The Easter Sermon" (ca. AD 400).

8. Fr. Bill Uren, "Seal of Confession Should Remain Inviolate," *Eureka Street* 27, no. 24 (2017), https://www.eurekastreet.com.au/article.aspx?aeid=54425.

9. John Henry Newman, "Letter to the Duke of Norfolk (1875)," in *The Genius of John Henry Newman: Selections from His Writings* (Oxford: Clarendon Press, 1989), 267.

10. Attributed to Fr. Pedro Arrupe (1907–91). See Kevin F. Burke, "Love Will Decide Everything: Pedro Arrupe Recovered the Ignatian 'Mysticism of Open Eyes,'" *America*, November 12, 2007.

5. Holy Orders

1. Anthony Kain, *Exploring the Sacraments: Appreciating God's Presence* (Collegeville, MN: Liturgical Press, 2006), 54–55.

2. Adrian Lyons, *Imagine Believing: Explorations in Contemporary Faith* (Melbourne, Australia: David Lovell, 2003), 185.

3. Elizabeth Johnson, "Redeeming the Name of Christ: Christology," in *Freeing Theology*, ed. Catherine Mowry LaCugna (San Francisco: HarperCollins, 1993), 115–37.

4. Pope John Paul II, *Mulieris Dignitatem* (Rome: Libreria Editrice Vaticana, 1988), http://w2.vatican.va/content/john-paul-ii/en/apost_letters/1988/documents/hf_jp-ii_apl_19880815_mulieris-dignitatem.html.

5. Emil A. Wcela, "Why Not Women? A Bishop Makes a Case for Expanding the Diaconate," *America*, October 1, 2012, http://americamagazine.org/issue/5152/article/why-not-women.

6. Joshua J. McElwee, "Vatican Spokesman: Female Cardinals 'Theoretically Possible,'" *National Catholic Reporter*, November 4, 2013,

http://ncronline.org/blogs/ncr-today/vatican-spokesperson-women
-cardinals-theoretically-possible.

7. Pope Francis, "Letter to His Eminence Cardinal Marc Armand
Ouellet, PSS" (Rome: Libreria Editrice Vaticana, 2016), https://w2
.vatican.va/content/francesco/en/letters/2016/documents/papa
-francesco_20160319_pont-comm-america-latina.html.

8. Pope Francis, "Clericalism Exploits the Law and Tyrannises
the People," *Vatican Insider*, December 13, 2016, http://www.lastampa
.it/2016/12/13/vaticaninsider/eng/the-vatican/clericalism-exploits
-the-law-and-tyrannises-the-people-fAEObUlnXNVJ18IpbjTAcO/
pagina.html.

9. Pope Francis, "Pope: Clericalism Distorts the Church," *Independent Catholic News*, April 26, 2016, https://www.indcatholicnews
.com/news.php?viewStory=29941.

10. Pope Francis, "Letter to His Eminence Cardinal Marc Armand
Ouellet, PSS," (Rome: Libreria Editrice Vaticana, 2016), https://w2
.vatican.va/content/francesco/en/letters/2016/documents/papa
-francesco_20160319_pont-comm-america-latina.html.

6. Marriage

1. Jonathan Sacks, "'The Love that Brings New Life into the
World'—Rabbi Sacks on the Institution of Marriage," November 17,
2014, http://rabbisacks.org/love-brings-new-life-world-rabbi-sacks
-institution-marriage/.

2. Sacks, "'The Love that Brings New Life into the World.'"

3. John R. Donahue, "A People of the Covenant," *America*, June
17, 2000, 38, https://www.americamagazine.org/content/the-word/
people-covenant.

4. Raymond E. Brown, "The Johannine Sacramentary Reconsidered," *Theological Studies* 23, no. 2 (1962): 183–206.

5. Joseph Martos, *Doors to the Sacred: A Historical Introduction to Sacraments in the Christian Church* (Liguori, MO: Liguori Publications, 2014), 415.

6. Elizabeth Clark, *St. Augustine on Marriage and Sexuality* (Washington, DC: Catholic University of America Press, 1996), 4.

7. Lisa Sowle Cahill, "Marriage," in *Commentary on the Catechism of the Catholic Church*, ed. Michael J. Walsh (Collegeville, MN: Liturgical Press, 1994), 328.

8. Jack Dominian, "'God Is Love': A Commentary on Benedict XVI's Encyclical," *The Furrow* 57, no. 5 (May 2006): 284–85.

9. Peter Steinfels, "Beliefs: A Study of Medieval Rituals in Same-Sex Unions Raises a Question; What Were They Solemnizing?" *The New York Times*, June 11, 1994.

10. Archbishop Joseph E. Kurtz, "Supreme Court Decision on Marriage a Tragic Error," U.S. Conference of Catholic Bishops, June 26, 2015.

7. Anointing of the Sick and Funerals

1. Letter Si Institutu Ecclesiastica, chap. 8: PL, 20, 559–61; Denz.-Schon, 216, as cited in Pope Pius VI, *The Sacrament of the Anointing of the Sick*, 1972, n. 2, http://www.papalencyclicals.net/paul06/p6anoin.htm.

2. Kevin W. Irwin, *Context and Text: Method in Liturgical Theology* (Collegeville, MN: Pueblo Books, 1994), 327.

3. Brian Doyle, *Leaping: Revelations & Epiphanies* (Chicago: Loyola Press, 2013), 53.

4. Anthony Kain, *Exploring the Sacraments: Appreciating God's Presence* (Collegeville, MN: Liturgical Press, 2006), 50.

5. Johannes Baptist Metz, *Poverty of Spirit* (New York: Paulist Press, 1998), 12.

6. A traditional Gaelic blessing.